FUTURE PROOF

YOUR HOME

A Guide to Building with Energy Intelligence in Cold Climates

Volume 1

Shane Wolffe

P.Eng, LEED AP BD+C, CEA, Level 1 Thermographer

www.futureproofmybuilding.com

March 21, 2013

Version 1.0

Print copy ISBN 978-0-9918281-1-1

About the Author

 Born and raised in Prince Albert, SK, Canada, Shane received his bachelor's degree from the University of Regina, specializing in Electronic Systems Engineering. As a registered Professional Engineer (Saskatchewan), LEED (Leadership in Energy and Environmental Design), Accredited Professional in Building Design and Construction, Certified Energy Auditor and Certified Level One Thermographer, Shane uses his skills to advance the practice of commissioning in both buildings and industrial processes. Shane founded Future Proof Commissioning Solutions Inc./Future Proof Software Solutions Ltd. with the objective of helping society by promoting the practice of commissioning, educating the public about energy saving/renewable technologies and preparing society for the uncertainties of tomorrow.

Shane's career began as a Programmer Analyst for Saskatchewan Government Insurance. Driven by his passion for the environment, Shane found a job with Honeywell Building Solutions where he worked as an Automation Technician, performing preventative maintenance and service work in over 50 buildings spanning multiple facility types, including hospitals, schools, office buildings, care homes, post-secondary institutions, malls, recreation facilities, pools and even a science center with a live butterfly hatchery.

This led to a project management position at Integrated Designs Inc. where Shane learned how to assist owners and project teams to ensure project success through the

1

implementation of the commissioning process. It was here that Shane project managed and performed the commissioning of several large construction projects, including the Dubé Center for Mental Health, Humboldt Hospital, Credit Union Center (re-commissioning), and several LEED projects including Meadow Lake Provincial Court House, The Red Deer Royal Canadian Mounted Police detachment, and the Moose Jaw Multiplex among several others. This experience has also reached into the industrial realm with the commissioning of the Raw Water pumping station for the City of Saskatoon and the commissioning of the Buffalo Pound Water Pumping Station North project.

Shane is in the process of partnering with Habitat for Humanity Saskatoon to implement the commissioning process for affordable home construction. By combining his knowledge of energy efficiency and the commissioning process, Shane is set to demonstrate that highly efficient housing can be constructed in a cost-effective manner if the proper mindset is implemented. Of significant importance is that this will be accomplished in Saskatoon, a city with one of the harshest climates and fastest growing populations in North America.

ABOUT THE ADVISOR

Robert S. Dumont, Ph.D. is essentially Jedi Master Yoda when it comes to energy efficiency. For this reason, many of the techniques discussed in this publication are directly derived from or related to his knowledge and expertise.

Dumont has been working with energy efficiency since the early 1970s. He was involved with the development of the Saskatchewan Conservation House, Canada's first low-energy house incorporating passive solar, active solar and super-insulated construction. Many of the techniques used in this project were then copied and used in Europe to create the ultra-low energy Passive House standard (Passivhaus in German), which is used widely in Europe and is considered by many to be the best standard in the world for ensuring energy efficiency in construction projects.

From 1974 to 1975, Dumont also helped develop the first residential air-to-air heat exchanger in Canada. This is a device that is now widely implemented in residential construction projects in cold climates. Dumont has since sat on the Canadian Standards Association Committee for Mechanical Ventilation.

From 1979 to 1990 Dumont worked as an Associate Research Officer for the Institute for Research in Construction and the National Research Council, specializing in energy conservation, air leakage and air quality in buildings where he performed surveys of the airtightness of residential buildings and helped develop air tightness guidelines for new construction. Dumont co-developed the residential energy analysis software program HOTCAN, now known as the HOT-2000 program. This program is used extensively for modeling construction projects to determine their energy requirements.

From 1990 to the present Dumont has worked as a researcher and consultant specializing in building energy efficiency, building envelopes, indoor air quality and indoor environment research. This involved a wide range of energy efficiency activities including commercial, institutional and residential building energy audits, integrated design of new institutional buildings for energy efficiency, whole building air tightness tests, standards development work for housing agencies including the National Building Code of Canada, Saskatchewan Housing Corporation, demonstration projects including the Canadian Advanced Houses Program, the Saskatchewan Advanced House, and the Factor 9 Home. Dumont's own house in Saskatoon was built in 1992 and was considered the best insulated house in the world for several years, having been measured to use 85 percent less energy than a standard construction home.[1] Rob is also the designer responsible for the VerEco home, which aims to become the first net zero home in Saskatchewan.

Rob has written over 50 publications in the areas of Energy Efficiency, Indoor Air Quality and Solar energy. He has also received several awards, including Solar Person of the Year 1988, the 1998 Bright Award for Innovation, and the Canadian Home Builders' Association 1998 William M. McCance Award for outstanding contributions to the Canadian housing industry in the technical area. To sum it up, Rob knows his stuff.

CONTENTS

Introduction

WHY SHOULD I CARE ABOUT HAVING AN EFFICIENT HOME?

HOW DID WE MAKE OURSELVES DEPENDENT?

We live in a changing world where the only real certainty at the moment is that energy prices from traditional sources will rise and things have the potential to get better or get worse. In a world where scientists have been telling us for decades that climate change is occurring and is man-made, many people lament and wonder what they can do to make things better other than recycling, driving less (or more efficiently) and making smart buying decisions. The reality is that a construction boom is happening in the prairies at the moment, and it brings with it the potential for great ecological and economic opportunity.

This book is written with the intention to give YOU the consumer the power and knowledge that you need in order to get the highest efficiency home for the lowest cost from your builder. You see, I'm not an expert in the intricacies of the building code, but I can tell you one thing – the building code in Canada is not designed for the climate in the Prairie Provinces, and as many efficiency experts would argue, the majority of Canada.

This is because when it comes to the building code concerning insulation (R-value[2]), the code is the LOWEST standard that must be met to avoid breaking the law.

Why is this exactly? ***The current building code allows you to build any assembly you want as long as you can keep the insides warm.*** In other words energy efficiency has traditionally never been part of the building code of Canada. Hence, houses and other buildings being built today are being built to a standard that doesn't care how much energy is consumed by the building over its lifetime.[3] When you consider that buildings consume the most energy per sector in North America, it is essentially a no-brainer as to why.

The good news is that a certain level of energy efficiency is required with the upcoming changes to the existing code. This level of efficiency is determined by the number of "heating degree days" of a particular area or region.[4] Though this new energy code has yet to be legislated anywhere in Canada, this is a huge improvement over the voluntary efficiency standards that are currently in place. However, the problem is that the provinces have the option as to whether or not they will adopt the model energy code provisions or not. Such a decision will definitely affect the economic direction that a particular region will take over the long term and hence will determine the resulting energy dependence of the population within that region. This is one of the primary reasons that I have spent several years and many unpaid weeks of my life learning and compiling this information in order to write this book. People need to know this information before our society takes a path from which it is very difficult and extremely costly to turn back... namely, the path of continued fossil fuel dependence.

On the international stage, Canadians (and in particular, Western Canadians) get the finger pointed at them for having a very high carbon footprint per capita in comparison to the rest of the world's citizens. Given the information above, there should be little doubt as to why this is the case.

It is worth noting that past legislators throughout Canada could have chosen to improve this standard and make it into law many years ago to reduce our society's energy dependence. This has been proven in places with higher energy costs such as Sweden, where in the 1970s the government stepped in and legislated much greater energy efficiency in new construction than is currently only suggested in Canada.[5] If our leaders had the same foresight as those of less energy-rich countries, our current dependence on fossil fuels and rankings on the world stage in terms of efficiency would be far more heartening. Our voluntary compliance with regard to energy code, combined with our extreme climate, is one of the top reasons that Canada has ranked second last of the 12 nations studied to evaluate energy efficiency.[6]

While a policy to ensure a higher standard of energy efficiency would be the best solution towards combating climate change and reducing our dependence on fossil fuels, it seems that the push will have to come from elsewhere. My intent is that by familiarizing yourself with the content in this book, *citizens and consumers* will now have the power, and will choose to exercise the power to personally implement or direct their hired designer or builder to implement techniques that will greatly reduce their individual (and our collective) dependency on fossil fuels.

The statement above might sound revolutionary, but think about it. If you live in any of the Prairie Provinces or territories, you are among the 1 percent of the world's population that lives in the coldest inhabited climate on earth! If you live anywhere in Canada, you are among the top 3 percent.[7]

To gain a broader perspective on the topic, consider that the national building code is a standard that was written for the majority of Canada in a time when energy costs were low and global warming was not an issue. At that time, the price of added insulation was more costly than simply burning some gas, oil or wood for heat. This standard has since evolved slowly as conditions have changed, but unfortunately it is still way behind for the current world conditions.

So why don't we just legislate vast improvements immediately? While that is the ultimate solution, the problem is that there is a lack of the skilled industry knowledge and expertise that is necessary to ensure compliance with such legislation. Essentially, with the current labour and market conditions, the codes can't evolve too fast or changes would potentially overwhelm many professionals within the industry, such as inspectors, contractors, designers, builders, etc. As such, the perceived risks that designers/builders face while undertaking projects increase due to the uncertainty that they now face. Such risks would undoubtedly be passed on to consumers and hence the price of housing/building stock would be prone to significant increases. This situation is even more complicated because politics are involved.

Politicians are elected by the people within an area to represent local interests and are expected to work in the best interest of constituents to move society forward in a positive manner. Although many builders and designers would be happy to build more efficient structures, being required to do so is another matter. In other words, when a legislator tries to change the code drastically, they are basically adding complication and cost to an established practice, making it more likely that they will lose their jobs. Consequently, most politicians who are not looking at the changing dynamics of the world in years to come are not likely to push for such changes, as many people without the understanding in this book may be prone to revolt, seeing the changes as government interference. The reality is that continual innovation and efficiency should be the goal of a progressive and mature society.

When you combine this dilemma with the large revenues that are generated for the government by the fossil fuel industry, there is little doubt as to why change happens much slower than is necessary to combat the current environmental situation regarding energy. Thus it is up to innovators and forward thinking citizens (like you) to push the envelope and try to influence others while the majority continues on its present course with business as usual. Thus, even with recent proposed improvements to the code, the energy usage of our buildings is still much higher than is necessary and this is mainly a result of the low consumer price of natural gas.

WE ARE BEING DUPED

Consider what artificially low prices for fossil fuel (in this case natural gas) translates to in the big picture. Even though the gas used to heat most of our buildings is clean-burning and still relatively cheap to purchase, if you consider its true cost due to what economists call "externalities," natural gas, along with the other fossil fuels on which we depend, are extremely expensive. This topic necessitates a book in itself, but I refer to, in particular, our dependence on a commodity that is prone to price volatility; our tax dollars going towards subsidizing its extraction and usage; and damage to the environment, which in terms of real dollars can often not even be quantified due to water pollution, air pollution, smog and direct contribution to global warming. On a societal level one should also consider the barrage of plastic and dispensable junk products that are refined from the extraction of petrochemicals, perpetuating a throw-away mentality toward most consumer goods in the majority of the population. But the real issue that should be on the minds of all citizens is the insane use of taxpayer dollars towards the subsidization of the most profitable and polluting industry in the world: namely, the fossil fuel industry. In 2011 the worldwide transfer of wealth from energy dependent citizen to excessively profitable corporation was estimated to be in excess of $523 billion dollars, with $3 billion of those tax payer dollars coming from Canadians.[8]

Without digressing further from the topic of buildings, consider that the national building code was once applicable across Canada. Hence, what was acceptable in Vancouver was also acceptable in Saskatoon. While this is no longer true due to recent improvements, one must ask the question: how can a standard that works in a more temperate climate such as Vancouver, BC (whose average January low temperature is 3°C and yearly average temperature is 11.0°C) or Toronto (whose average January low temperature is -7°C and yearly average temperature is 9.2°C) apply to a place like Saskatoon whose average January low temperature is -22°C and yearly average temperature 2.6°C?[9]

The short answer is that this standard isn't sufficient for the climate in which we live, nor for the world in which we live. If you don't believe me, try turning off your furnace or source of heat for a few hours in the middle of winter. But why stop there? Try it in the spring or fall and see how long it takes for your house to become uncomfortably cold. You can also try this test by turning off your air conditioning in the heat of the summer and you will likely notice that most buildings are readily prone to overheating due to heat migration through the structure.[10] Logically, one should assume that no matter where you live; *your house should be sufficiently insulated to retain enough heat that it does not require an external energy source other than the sun during the average yearly temperature in order to stay reasonably comfortable.*[11]

While this is not always possible due to site restrictions and the extreme nature of some climates, it can be done reasonably well even in extreme climates like that of the Canadian prairies. Based on this test, my guess is that unless your house was built with the energy crisis of the 1970s in mind, most people's biggest investment (their house) is dependent on cheap and abundant natural gas, fuel oil or electricity in the middle of winter in order to keep it comfortable and prevent its plumbing from freezing. Unfortunately, this means that such a facility will not protect your family or the plumbing in your house in the dead of winter if the worst were to happen.

THE IMPLICATIONS MOUNT

This means that for most of us, the only way that we can live in Canada is to use a large amount of energy to offset the shortcomings of the undersized "buffer" of an exterior wall. This scares me for several reasons, but here are the biggest:

1. We are (in most cases) completely dependent on the consumption of a limited resource, which is directly responsible for climate change. I am referring to natural gas or coal, which is used to create heat and/or electricity. These two substances by their very nature are prone to variations in price, which puts us at the mercy of a world market that does not care whether or not we can afford this commodity. This is particularly true when one considers the true cost of these energy sources due to subsidies and environmental damage, as discussed previously.

2. The Prairie Provinces and Territories are seeing massive economic growth at the moment, causing developers to build structures at an incredible rate.[12] Most of these developers will do so to satisfy demand for housing and commercial real estate in a manner that meets their clients' requirements and is most cost-effective for them. This is not their fault; they are in business to make money and will try to make the most

of it that they can while still meeting their customers' requirements and not breaking the law. While this makes sense from a strictly "now" and "first cost economics perspective," it's concerning because most people simply do not realize that a building (house, apartment, mall etc.) is a long-term investment in the price and availability of energy needed to operate and maintain that facility. When a building is constructed, the makeup of the building exterior or "building envelop" at the time of construction is essentially the determining factor for the amount of energy that it will consume over its entire lifetime. Furthermore, it is far cheaper to build it correctly and with energy efficiency in mind in the first place than to try to retrofit after the fact. As Mike Holmes says, "Make it right."

3. The consumption of these fossil fuels is directly related to climate change, which creates uncertainty on a global scale by affecting everything from weather patterns, to the durability of our infrastructure, to food production. As many experts have been saying for many years now, this is a direct safety concern that affects the entire human race, both now and for future generations to come.[13]

You may be sceptical of this statement, but regardless of your knowledge concerning the issue of climate change, one thing is certain; *we will always be better off consuming less fossil fuel, both financially and in terms of pollution (whether created in the air, water or soil as a result of extracting, refining and transporting energy from traditional sources).*[14] This is especially true when one considers the inevitable price increases and decreasing supply. Sadly, our society has become so obsessed with supplementing this supply that we are drilling for oil and gas in some of the most environmentally sensitive and dangerous places in the world: namely, the middle of the Arctic Ocean.

WHAT WE CAN DO TO IMPROVE OUR BUILDINGS

"Begin with the end in mind."
Steven Covey – Habit #2 of "The 7 Habits of Highly Effective People"

When it comes to being efficient, the primary decisions must be made before a lot is even considered to build on. If one considers that *a home—or any building, for that matter—is a system*, the decisions required to make the building efficient are more obvious. With this mindset and the principles listed below, the process is simplified:

1. Remember that the building is a system and consider how shifting the costs to improve one area of the building can reduce the need to spend money on other components/systems within the building.

2. Properly insulating a home in a cold or moderate climate is by far the cheapest method of ensuring energy efficiency. Not requiring energy for heating or cooling may permit a smaller size of heating or cooling equipment or even remove the need for such equipment altogether (this typically saves money on the equipment and ongoing cost of operation) and is far more cost-effective than producing energy with renewable energy—at least for the time being.[15]

3. The building must be properly sealed to ensure that air is not leaking into or out of the building in an uncontrolled manner.

4. The building must be properly ventilated to ensure that occupants have access to clean air and to prevent the accumulation of humidity and growth of mold. This is highly important for the health and safety of occupants, particularly in a well-sealed or super-insulated building.

5. The building should be facing south (in the northern hemisphere) with adequate windows and properly placed shading to take advantage of passive solar gains in the winter and reduce unnecessary heat gains in the summer. This is called passive solar design and is a consideration that must be made prior even to selecting the lot, in some cases.

6. Using too many windows or using windows that are excessively large creates a significant source of energy loss in the winter and of heat gain in the summer.

7. Heat gain in the summer is particularly a problem on the east, west and south sides of a building, especially if the windows are not shaded.

8. A smaller home requires less energy than a bigger home due to reduced surface area exposed to the exterior conditions.

9. Light coloured roofing and siding will greatly reduce the need for cooling in the summer and have little effect with regard to capturing heat energy in the winter.

10. Thermal mass within the home can be cost-effective in mitigating temperature swings and is very useful for capturing heat in passive solar homes.

11. High-efficiency equipment for heating and cooling will save significant money on energy costs over their lifetime.

12. Reusing energy through energy recovery ventilators or drain water heat recovery takes advantage of the energy that has already been paid for.

13. The usage of energy-efficient lighting and appliances is a good way to reduce your energy consumption year round. This principle can easily be applied after a home is constructed.

14. Monitoring occupant behaviour has a significant effect on the usage of energy within any building. This principle can easily be applied after a home is constructed.

All of these concepts will be explored in greater detail later. It is fairly intuitive that pretty much all of these principles must be considered and implemented in the design and construction phases so as to be implemented in a cost-effective manner.

While there is obviously much more to the complexity of this system, by understanding and applying these principles in all situations, a very high level of energy efficiency can be achieved in virtually any building – and therefor across society. With that in mind, you may find it rather shocking that according to the Environmental Protection Agency (EPA), the USGBC and CaGBC (US and Canadian Green Building Councils) and other various organizations dedicated to energy research, buildings are responsible for approximately 40 percent of the total energy consumed in our society, and are therefore the highest source of greenhouse gas emissions in North America.

What makes this statistic most shocking is that a building is one of the only systems that can be designed to actually produce more energy than it consumes on a yearly average basis. Such a structure is the definition of a net zero building.

Think of how backwards this is! For all of these years we have prided ourselves on being an advanced species, while at the same time we have actually been manufacturing and feeding our dependence on a limited, expensive and polluting commodity by not doing things as well as we are able. It is as if we humans are asleep at the wheel and driving towards the cliff as fast as the car will go. Or more accurately, if you consider that certain interest groups are in control of the economy, these groups are driving us towards the cliff while trying to push the pedal further to the floor by refusing to address the problems that our fossil fuel addiction has created.[16]

Another interesting statistic from these same organizations is that North Americans spend 90 percent of their time in buildings. It is no wonder that there is such a push to "Build Green," considering that these buildings are the places in which we live, work, play and separate ourselves from the natural world.

The logical solution, it seems, would be to build each and every building to use as little energy as possible, or to build them to actually produce more than they consume and hence give back to the world. While this may sound costly and even foolish to some, when you consider that a building is a long-term asset that can have more uses than simply to house people, this idea has much more merit.

I'm not suggesting that everyone is able to or should try to build to net zero—at least not yet. The cost, availability and limitations of certain technologies and expertise necessary to make every new home or building a net zero facility are still out of reach. This is especially true in the coldest of climates. *However, it is possible to reduce the energy consumption within a home by as much as 85 percent using standard technology and documented building practices at little to no extra cost, if this is the goal from the beginning of the project. This is achievable today by simply changing the common mindset and implementing the ideas and technologies expressed in this book.*[17]

As Brendan Bouchard said, "the time to have the map is before you enter the woods." In order to make the proper decisions when planning a building, whether it is the owner or the designer, one must know how they are going to reach their destination before they even begin. If you are building a new home and you follow the suggestions posed in this book, then you will have built a home that is far more efficient than that of your neighbours. Furthermore, you (or the lucky person who buys your home) can be ready to cost–effectively make the move to net zero in the near future when the price of solar drops and you are able to produce your own electricity locally.

THE CASE FOR A SOLAR-POWERED
SOCIETY IN THE NEAR FUTURE

Based on most peoples knowledge of the solar industry, it will be a very long time before it is cost–effective to power ones home using renewable energy. However, with the proper steps taken, that is not the case. As is demonstrated in the figures below, the price and supply of solar have both changed exponentially according to a phenomenon known as Swanson's Law (very similar to Moore's law for computers, but slightly different to apply to the solar industry). By many estimates and depending on public demand, utility involvement and government action, replacing existing electrical capacity may be cost-effective compared to current infrastructure within eight years (by 2020). To quote a recent blog article in GreenBuildingAdvisor.com,[18] in some places in the United States it is already cost-effective to install solar power rather than pay for the existing electrical utility at current prices. This is especially true when you consider that "solar is falling in price approximately 7 percent per year while fuel prices increase 2 percent per year."

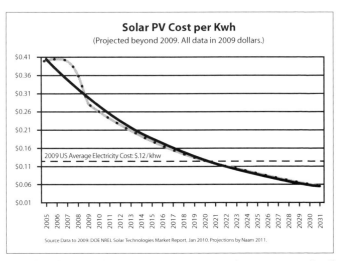

It won't be long until powering our society using the sun in virtually all markets is cost-effective.[19]

How long will it take for solar to be on par with current infrastructure in your area? That I can't answer because the power sources and their associated cost (hydro power vs. coal vs. nuclear vs. wind vs. natural gas etc.) vary greatly from region to region and provider to provider. In some regions, it may not be feasible or reasonable to ever change from the existing source based on first cost and simplicity alone. Given that the electrical infrastructure in most regions is currently based on a centralized power production model, future issues concerning erratic weather patterns such as was witnessed during hurricane Sandy may be the factor that pushes utilities towards decentralized power networks that incorporate Smart Grids. A decentralized model will not be without its headaches, costs and hiccups; however I believe that it is the way of the future.

In many people's minds, photovoltaic panels are still too expensive. Thankfully, this is changing rapidly thanks to new technology and innovation. However, the spread of such technology would be best accomplished through more widespread implementation. To achieve this, people will need to accept this information, and old-school thinking on the subject of energy and economics will need to change.

Since it doesn't intuitively make sense that a technology can get cheaper so rapidly, a good way to understand the rapid advances in solar is to consider how fast the computer took off (according to Moore's Law). Think about it this way, how much did a top-of-the-line computer cost and what was its computing capacity just 10 years ago, 20 years ago? The same exponential cost reductions are occurring right now in the "Cost per Watt of Solar PV (Photo Voltaic)" and "Watts Produced per Constant $100" in the photovoltaic industry.[20] When one compares these numbers to the implementation of the computer, the outlook for solar is very good considering that the end user does not need to learn how to use a solar panel the way they needed to learn to use a computer: a professional can install the panel.

Not only are photovoltaics getting cheaper; they are also starting to be integrated into windows and other construction materials. This makes the area available to collect power much larger than simply on the rooftops and in fields. When coupled with the recent advances in battery technology and combine that with the Smart Grid (an innovation which will produce many jobs and opportunities for the advancement and security of society), then we have a very clean and dependence free road map that will help us move to net zero,[21] create thousands of high-paying local jobs and allow us to breath cleaner air and have healthier waterways, all at the same time.

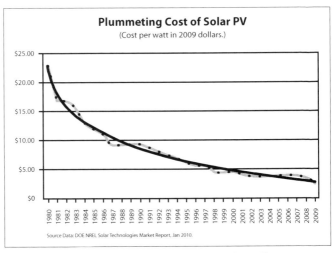

The cost and availability of solar just keeps getting better.[22]

YOU CAN DO IT

While I haven't yet discussed the efficiency measures that will make building to net zero feasible, I want to point out that efficiency is by far the cheapest manner by which we can reduce our dependence on fossil fuels. I have included the discussion of solar above to demonstrate that with the proper first steps, which will be discussed soon, we can meet net zero in the near future by producing our own energy from an unlimited source. Taking all of these steps sends a powerful message to government that we as a society want to live in a clean future, a future that does not require the consumption of power from dirty sources.

By improving our homes and buildings we have the greatest potential to reduce our environmental impact. And since *the only vote we truly cast in this society is with our dollars, every move we make towards this goal has the highest impact while setting a positive example for others.*

I'M NOT SOLD YET. WHY DOES THIS AFFECT ME?

"Change is not necessary because survival is optional."
W.Edward Demming

If you are building a home, you are probably wondering: why is this of concern to me at this time? First of all, there is climate change, which is already proving to change the weather patterns that we have come to depend on for our food, shelter and even safety. With any increases in erratic weather, and the strength at which this weather impacts the earth, come inherent problems if and when they affect our infrastructure. There are numerous examples of this all over the world lately, but one that hits close to home occurred all over Saskatchewan in the summer of 2012 where thousands of people were without power for several days. In Prince Albert a small city of 50,000, the entire city was affected and only one gas station in the entire city was able to operate during the outage. This caused a lineup of vehicles several blocks long and demonstrates perfectly our dependence on both reliable power and access to fossil fuels. [23]

The circumstances weren't as severe in Canada as in the eastern United States during the summer of 2012, where heat waves and power outages caused millions of dollars of food to spoil and even caused deaths from heat exhaustion. Take it a step further and you see how on July 31, 2012 in India an estimated 670 million people were without power, many of them for several days. Such situations demonstrate how dependent our society is on electricity to run our lives.

Imagine the consequences if such a scenario were to play out in the middle of winter such as what happened from January 5 to 10, 1998 in Ontario, Quebec and New Brunswick.[24] During that ice storm, more than 4.5 million Canadians were without power. In some areas, the outage lasted for an entire month. The consolation in this situation is that the weather in Ontario, Quebec and New Brunswick doesn't get nearly as cold as in the prairies. Though it was the most expensive disaster in Canadian history, such a situation would be much more serious in a colder climate. If such an outage were to occur again, many people would lose the plumbing in their homes and businesses when pipes froze. But given that people (not knowing the dangers of carbon monoxide) have died while operating their barbeques indoors without ventilation, freezing pipes are small tragedies by comparison.

While extreme weather disrupting infrastructure is an extreme example, an example which we have seen multiple times in Western Canada during the winter of 2012 to 2013, consider how our homes are heated in the winter. For most people in the prairies, our heat comes from natural gas. Combine this with our less-than-ideal building envelopes means that *our extreme climate makes us extremely dependent on the price of natural gas.* While this commodity is quite cheap at the moment, we are at a time when the world is changing rapidly and new power options are becoming available, so this will affect us.

Though I am not an expert in economics or in the area of natural gas reserves, I do believe that the price will go up substantially in the coming years for a number of reasons:

1. Natural gas is seen as a bridge fuel for moving the current electrical grid infrastructure over to renewable energy. While this is a good thing in terms of moving away from its dirtier cousin coal, this means that several natural gas plants are being constructed all over the world that will undoubtedly increase the demand and hence the price of natural gas.

2. The United States economy has been quite slow since the recession of 2008, which has reduced the demand for natural gas significantly. If the economy picks up again, the price of this commodity will as well.

3. Many bus and car fleets are turning towards natural gas as a clean-burning alternative to gasoline or diesel. The market of natural gas powered cars and buses are expected to grow by 14 percent and 19 percent respectively by 2019.[25] While this is a step in the right direction to reduce our dependence on oil, it will undoubtedly increase the demand and hence the price of natural gas.

4. In light of the devastation caused by the tsunamis in Japan in March of 2011, the Japanese have indicated that they will be moving away from nuclear power in favour of renewable and natural gas electrical generation. It is likely that other jurisdictions will follow suit and hence will affect the price.[26]

5. The practice of shale gas fracking in the United States has produced a large amount of excess natural gas on the market, which has brought the price down to the low levels that we see today. This practice has been linked to many environmental problems and is currently under review by several government agencies in the Northeastern United States. This is because there is significant fear about how shale gas fracking could affect the Pennsylvania watershed, which feeds New York City as well as several other large cities in the Northeastern United States. If you would like to learn more about this, I recommend the documentary *Gasland* which is available on Netflix or the Internet. Alternatively there are many articles on the subject. [27]

Many investors with interests in natural gas will consider price increases to be a good thing; however, the fact remains that burning natural gas releases CO_2 and natural gas is primarily composed of methane, which makes it 20 times as potent as CO_2[28] when it escapes into the atmosphere. Therefore, it is my opinion that natural gas would be best left under the earth's surface where it cannot further alter the atmospheric conditions that have allowed the biodiversity of life on our planet to flourish. Whether or not you agree with this, it is hard to argue that as people living in one of the coldest places on earth, we as a society and as individuals would be better off if we were less dependent on this commodity, both financially and in regards to protecting the environment.

BUT GAS IS CHEAP

With all of this in mind, skeptics will say that the "economy already uses this commodity," "the infrastructure is already in place" and "it's expected to stay low for several years." Without using the price of oil as a benchmark it's hard to logically conclude that the price of a finite resource will stay at a low price… regardless of what markets predict. Never mind that natural gas is a fossil fuel and hence is directly responsible for climate change. But it all comes down to the almighty dollar, which seems to be the most important factor for decision-makers regarding the manner by which they heat or cool buildings.

One can't argue with gas being an economical heating option at the moment. But as I illustrated above, the price is very likely to rise. How much exactly? Does it really matter in terms of how you choose to spend your money now? Will the fear of a price increase of 2, 3, 5, or 10 times of the current price be the factor that makes you choose efficiency over hoping for stability? If you consider that in the future your money will lose value due to the nature of money itself, is it not more reasonable to invest in sheltering yourself from being economically affected in the future by spending more of today's dollars to increase the value of your biggest asset—your home? Also keep in mind: given that your money will lose value over time due to inflation, any potential energy upgrades to your home in the future will also undoubtedly cost more money to implement in terms of today's dollars, because implementing efficiency after a building is constructed is extremely expensive.[29]

Before you write off this discussion of price volatility as sheer speculation, consult the info-graphic below showing that the price of natural gas was over four times its current value (approximately \$3/MMBTU[30] as of September 2012) in both 2008 (\$13/MMBTU) and 2005 (\$14/MMBTU). Further to this, if we look at the Enbridge natural gas price to consumers from January 2006 – March 2006, they were as 41.19 cents/m³ (and 41.67 cents/m³ in Union gas territory). In contrast to current natural gas prices in Enbridge, which are 8.81 cents/m³, we have seen a 367% swing in price between 2006 and 2012.

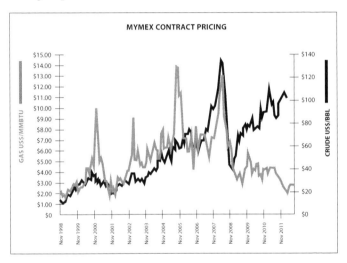

Historical fluctuations of natural gas prices in MMBTU.[31]

Did most consumers notice these price increases at those high points? Not likely, if you weren't paying attention or you use a low volume of natural gas. If the consumers themselves were not paying this price, then this is likely the result of subsidization stepping in to reduce the impact that most of us would feel as a result of an increase. If this is the case, then not only are our public funds diverted from important activities (such as health care, education, public service, or better infrastructure) to shelter us from a dependency that we have created, but now the dependency is essentially hidden from us at the same time. Hence, our dependency increases.

When one considers that this commodity that most of us completely rely on for heating our homes and businesses is prone to price fluctuations by its very nature, it should become obvious that we must reduce our dependence on it.

So, what if everyone took steps to reduce their dependence on energy? There is no doubt that this is desirable for utility companies, as reducing demand is far cheaper than building excess capacity, particularly if the excess capacity is for electrical generation. This is why programs such as the EcoEnergy Retrofit Programs for Homes exist. Such programs have the additional effect of improving the local economy in every area in which they are implemented. Though I am not particularly in favour of subsidies, I believe that these types of programs are a far better investment if the governments are to subsidize any activity, because the program affects all economies in all areas of the country. Not only does this economic activity save money for the consumer who takes advantage of it, but it also frees up the commodity (formerly subsidized for local use) to be sold to a foreign market.

By selling our natural resources, such as natural gas, by way of export, this activity brings capital into the territory of the producer and is a wise move economically if the commodity is in demand in other markets. In other words, if we don't use the gas ourselves, we can export it and bring money into the country, but this is even better if we don't have to import the commodity as it keeps money within our country. If the commodity is locally owned, then exporting it has the best potential economic benefits to our country, but given that the majority of our gas reserves are bought out by foreign investors, exporting the commodity has less benefit to the country, as the money goes to the owners of the resource. In other words, the owners of the resource simply want customers for their product, and as people who live in the cold for most of the year, we are great customers who have to pay someone else for our own resources. Not the smartest move, right?

Consider also how a widespread adoption of this efficiency mentality would reduce our society's dependence on fossil fuels and hence reduce the level of our indentured servitude via our jobs. On a grand scale, by having a much lower dependence, price increases become less of an issue across the board as subsidizing to remove the burden of high prices would become less necessary. So not only does efficiency save money for the taxpayer (and hence free up public funds for more important things), but I, for one, would be happy that our government would be reducing its support of the fossil fuel industry.

THE BIG PICTURE

Taking all of this into account, consider how each and every single new construction project is just a small piece of the puzzle. With every new build that is consuming energy, we are adding to the demand and hence putting strain on the existing system, be it an electrical delivery infrastructure or gas delivery infrastructure.[32] Never mind that during all of this, new resources must be discovered, extracted, refined and consumed; at some point, the existing infrastructure system needs to be expanded, and it costs money, either to the tax payer or to the local utility, to make this happen. In either scenario, the costs will be passed on to the consumer, who then needs to work more in order to pay for all of this expansion. When fully considered, this portion of the economy is like a tumor that just keeps growing and growing with nothing to stop it other than its own flawed nature of intended perpetual growth.

Consider now that every new build (shown with a dot in the graph below) was made to use very little energy or even to produce more energy than it consumes. If we were to look at this on a societal level, it would look something like this:

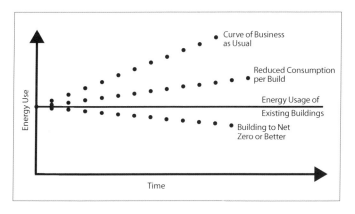

An illustration of how each new building built in a particular area adds to the energy necessary for that area.

While this chart is by no means meant to display the usage in a particular location, nor is it an all-inclusive account of all of the factors involved in our societies energy usage, it illustrates my point. Imagine that at a given rate of growth to reflect the slope of the growth lines, a standard size building uses 100 units of energy.[33] Every new building adds to the total amount of energy that is required within our society. The "Curve of Business as Usual" line in the illustration above represents the 100 units per building. Imagine, now, that as we move forward as a society, every new building is 75 percent more efficient. This scenario would be represented by the "Reduced Consumption per Build" line; not quite as good as Rob Dumont's house, but very achievable.

Such a scenario produces a much lesser strain on the existing infrastructure within a given location and on society as a whole, while also reducing the need to create more electrical and gas infrastructure to satisfy the growing demand. If there is less demand for the infrastructure needed to deliver fossil fuel energy, then all of the government subsidies that are given to these projects (and even investors who are putting their money into these oil and gas projects with the hope of high financial returns) could then put their money into improving the existing infrastructure or building stock of their local communities[34] or into their next construction project, perhaps for an office building or retail location.

While this may not make sense generally based on financial returns, consider how much your investments lost value during the market crash of 2008. Now consider how much control you had over that investment at that time, or at any time for that matter. When one considers all of the parties involved in manipulating the global economy, it makes me wonder why I would sink money into an investment that I have no control over. For this reason, I would say that it is a better idea to invest in the local economy of efficiency. In my opinion, not only is this far more ethical in terms of reducing the environmental impact of our societies growth, but it is a much safer investment as the improvements to one's own property allow the investor a much higher level of control over how an investment is spent on improving the value of the asset created, hence ensuring payback and creating a much higher level of personal/business security.

This scenario has the added bonus of encouraging a healthy local economy by creating local jobs and demonstrating a level of leadership to fellow citizens. One could argue that the publicity or stature gained from demonstrating such levels of leadership (both in a personal and a corporate sense) are of much higher value than the uncertain and fluctuating financial returns that most investors seek via external investments. Though the returns might not be as high financially, if status and ethics are of concern, then there couldn't be a much better win-win investment than building to net zero or improving the existing infrastructure and building stock to these levels, or as close as possible to these levels. Such an optimistic scenario would create the "Building to Net Zero or Better" line and be one of the fastest and most economically stimulating methods plausible to solving the problem of climate change.

The "Building to Net Zero or Better" line scenario is essentially the only way in which construction can be truly sustainable.

Chapter 1
SO HOW DO WE GET THERE?

"We cannot solve our problems with the same level of thinking that created them."
Albert Einstein

So how does one cost–effectively build toward net zero if you live in the most energy-hungry area of the world? First, we have to recognize that North American society is incredibly inefficient (particularly in sparsely populated areas), and then design our buildings and society in ways that promote and create higher efficiency. But how does one do that?

First of all I should state that even though this book is about building an efficient house, houses and sprawl are not the ways that society will ultimately improve in its efficiency. *Only by strategically increasing urban density through high rises and urban infill will our society be able to better improve its efficiency and sense of community.* While building community and reducing energy usage may seem idealistic and necessary, I acknowledge that in Western Canada we are in the middle of a booming economy and hence many people want their own house for living and raising their families because of the status and entitlement mentality that has been ingrained within us. In doing so, it is most wise to ensure that these dwellings are comfortable, healthy, long-lasting and energy-efficient in order to protect your family and wallet.

To explain every facet of how to accomplish this in great detail is not necessary and would not be possible in a book that is meant to educate you about how to understand and achieve efficiency. Improving efficiency essentially comes down to three principles:

1. **Reducing** the need for energy is much cheaper and easier than producing your own energy in most locations (at least for the time being). In a home, the cheapest and easiest opportunities for efficiency improvement come by reducing the requirements for space heating, water heating and electricity usage.

2. **Reusing** energy via methods such as heat recovery ventilators or through drain water heat recovery. Storing energy by implementing thermal mass is also very effective.

3. **Generating or harvesting** energy via creative design and renewable energy such as passive solar, solar thermal water and air heating, photovoltaic and ground source heat pumps (geothermal).

While this sounds quite complicated and difficult, if you use the right resources it becomes relatively simple to understand. If you want to understand how to achieve a comfortable, healthy and energy-efficient house, one must lean on the expertise of the innovators of energy efficiency and on established standards: namely, Passive House (Passivhaus in German, the building efficiency standard in Europe); R2000 (a North American standard for energy efficiency); and LEED (or Leadership in Energy and Environmental Design, the standard for green buildings in North America). While each of these standards has its pros and cons, the principles of each demonstrate what is of importance. It is these standards that I summarize for you in this publication in regards to energy efficiency.

For homes in Canada, the R2000 standard is a great blueprint to follow in regards to providing the highest quality home. R2000 addresses the majority of concerns in buildings such as electrical consumption through better appliances, indoor air quality through proper ventilation and reduction of the toxic elements in our homes though the reduction of volatile organic compounds (VOCs). R2000 homes are also required to have follow-up inspections to verify that components and systems are installed and operating correctly. This process helps to ensure quality and hence provide the homeowner with a level of assurance that they will not have to deal with unexpected issues, expenses and inconveniences in the future. As a consulting engineer who has acted as a commissioning agent for many different buildings and systems, I can testify to the high importance of this activity in the construction process.

BUT IT COSTS TOO MUCH!

Whenever people are asked to go above and beyond the code or minimum standard, there are usually limiting factors. When it comes to energy efficiency, that barrier is almost always cost.

Before I get into the very reasonable economics of building efficiently, I would like to make a side note concerning the fact that many people will spend thousands of dollars on luxuries and features when purchasing a vehicle. While fuel efficiency in a vehicle is more important to some than to others, it is worth noting that all vehicle classes have efficiency ratings that they must meet, yet homes and other buildings currently do not. This is quite a conundrum, given that homes use much more energy than vehicles. Now consider that a car owner will actually spend very little time in that vehicle compared to their home or a building in which they work. Many people also like to think of their vehicle as an asset, when in reality most banks consider a vehicle as a liability because it will depreciate in a very short amount of time as opposed to gain value over time as a home is expected to. Finally, a vehicle is susceptible to being destroyed by other vehicles, while the risks associated with investing in your home are much lower by comparison.

In 1992, when Dr. Rob Dumont (the advisor to this book) built his house, it was verified as the best-insulated house in the world. Rather than building to what is still considered by most to be an efficient wall system, namely that of a 2x6 wood-framed exterior wall, Dumont chose to go with a double wall system (which is explained in detail later in Chapter 3).

By implementing double wall construction, Dumont's walls achieve an R-value of 60, which is by far superior compared to standard 2x6 construction. This is because a 2x6 framed wall provides a nominal insulation value of R20 for the insulated spaces using fiberglass or rock wool insulation. Because of thermal bridging, the actual R-value of the wall assembly is closer to R16, which is caused by the low R-value per inch of wood studs and the transfer of heat through those studs into imperfectly insulated wall cavities. The concepts of thermal bridging and R-value are described in detail later.

Since the double wall system used in Dumont's house eliminates thermal bridging in the wall while incorporating a much higher R-value, Dumont's house in Saskatoon has been verified as 85 percent more efficient than a regular house of the same square footage that is built according to standard practice. To put it into technical perspective, Dumont's house has a peak heat loss of 5kW when the outside temperature is -34°C. It is for this reason that Dumont decided to save on the cost of installing a furnace and paying a monthly connection fee for gas by instead installing much cheaper thermostatically controlled electric baseboard heaters. While this will cost more to operate per unit of heat than using conventional gas heating at the current cost of gas in Saskatchewan, Dumont's low demand means that photovoltaic panels could be implemented to offset his utility cost and the installed solar thermal heating system can offset his heating demand during the winter.[35]

Though Dumont's house's title of "best insulated house in the world" has since been bested by other energy-efficient projects; the point is that super-insulating a house really doesn't add significantly to the construction cost of a house.[36] In Dumont's case he chose to utilize staggered stud double wall construction for the following reasons:

1. 2x4's and cellulose insulation (recycled newsprint with a fire retardant) are cheap and readily available in Canada. Dumont selected cellulose due to its cost and good R-value per inch.

2. A double wall system can be customized to achieve a higher R-value than is available using insulated concrete forms or structurally insulated panels at a much lower cost.

3. Using wood and cellulose create a wall system that actually acts as a means of sequestering carbon as opposed to introducing it to the atmosphere, as is the case with refining Styrofoam from oil and using concrete (made of cement).

4. These materials, when used properly, have a high R-value and produce excellent sound attenuation (they insulate against noise).

5. These materials are made in Canada and hence have a low carbon footprint, meaning they don't travel far nor do they require excessive energy to manufacture.

6. A double wall system provides nice window sills, due to the thick walls, for displaying items or growing plants and herbs.

Large window sills create plenty of room to grow herbs or various plants within the home year round.

In 1992 when the home was built, the incremental cost of the wall insulation that Dumont used to upgrade from an R20 nominal wall to an R60 wall was only $4,620. The incremental cost of an R80 attic cost was $1,050 and basement floor of R35 cost $920. These small investments have definitely paid for themselves over time and will continue to do so for many years to come. To read an article about Dumont's home and its other features, visit: www.futureproofmybuilding.com/rob-dumont-housenotes/

Dumont has worked with the statistics of various construction techniques for several years now and has determined that any residential construction can be super-insulated to the same R-value as his house by adding as little as 5 percent to 10 percent to the capital cost of the house. *With this knowledge Dumont chose to super-insulate his house, an investment that pays him back with energy savings and a higher level of security 24/7/365, rather than spending the same amount of money to put bricks around the exterior wall.* This brings me to my next point.

WEALTHY PEOPLE INVEST THEIR MONEY, POOR PEOPLE CREATE LIABILITIES.

If you have read *Rich Dad Poor Dad* by Robert Kiyosaki and Sharon Lechter, or understand the concept of building wealth, then you will be familiar with this concept. Unfortunately, an understanding of wealth is a concept that many people in our society have yet to understand. This isn't anyone's fault per se; it is an oversight that many have accepted as the norm. Unfortunately, this is a norm that tends to be reinforced by marketing and the media which perpetuates itself in order to sell us things that we don't need. Regardless of why many people don't understand wealth, it is human nature to place more value in the look of something (or even someone) as of higher importance than the actual substance behind that thing. Unfortunately, it seems as if this is how we are wired, though it is short-sighted and often does not make things better for us.

I refer here to a type of thinking that is unfortunately all too pervasive in construction and housing. We tend to emphasize things that are "pretty" as opposed to things that are "functional." The unfortunate side of this is that *our opinions concerning what is pretty or stylish change over time*. Therefore, focusing on the pretty things within a home (such as countertops, curtains, cabinets, crown molding, oak finish, flooring, fancy doors etc.) often detracts from the substance that really matters. When we do this we not only add to the project cost, but we are likely to spend less on the things that save us money in the long term. Unfortunately, it makes sense from a societal point of view that this focus is part of the reason that we have been doing it wrong for so long. For example, consider the décor example below:

Someone paid big money to make this room look stylish, and they probably loved it for awhile. Does this investment pay you back or stand the test of time?[37]

When you look at this picture, remind yourself that at one time the majority of the population thought that this style was attractive. While tastes and preferences vary from person to person, what's "in" now is guaranteed to not be "in" down the road.

Personal style and aesthetic preferences change over time and hence the money spent on these amenities becomes a liability if they are the focus of the project. This is especially true when the ongoing costs of heating and cooling reduce the value of the home or the space is uncomfortable because it is too prone to heat gain or loss. This does not mean that aesthetics are not important, but rather aesthetic features should be of secondary concern as the true value of the building comes from having something that is well built, comfortable, pleasant to live in, and made of materials that don't slowly release their toxic components that poison your family or make you sick.

If you are building a house it is advisable to put more money into its efficiency so that the owner can *recoup the investment over time*. Not only is this better for the environment, but it also provides a level of energy security that you would not have otherwise. This security and recouping of costs truly defines an asset. The reason that this concept escapes many is because that which is behind the wall is invisible to the owner/buyer and because energy has traditionally been cheap.

BUT I WILL LOSE SQUARE FOOTAGE!

"Trying to be happy by accumulating possessions is like trying to satisfy hunger by taping sandwiches all over your body."
George Carlin

Unless you are building on a lot or location that does not have strict height and size requirements, the concern of losing floor space within the home due to thick walls may be an issue. However, there will be cases where having thick walls will actually provide you with more living space, as a furnace room may no longer be necessary due to the reduced heating demand of the building. Such situations are complicated yet demonstrate the engineering concept of a trade-off. In other words, one quality is sacrificed or exchanged for another quality. This is where one's own biases and judgments play the most important role.

I have cited the quote above because in our society the symbol to most people that they are "successful" or "well off " is the size of their home. While this may make sense in our consumerist economy, it certainly has its shortcoming. By having so much space to satisfy our individual needs, we have not only taken over much of the natural world and encroached on nature, but now we are further apart both socially and physically from our places of work and play, and thus we spend more time commuting in isolation. Not only does this cost us in terms of the free time in which we can do as we please, but now we are spending more free time and money on transportation. Keep in mind that our neighbours now have to spend more time in transit as well and with road congestion becoming a problem as sprawl increases this is likely why road rage and driving frustration are becoming more common. Such is the argument in favour of the densification of cities. But the drawbacks of continued expansion don't end there.

While everyone likes having space to do as they like, one must realize that *the bigger the house, the more money and hence energy it takes to keep that house at a comfortable temperature.* This is the root of the problem and is particularly true if your large house simply meets code or standard practice. This is why it is so important to think about how much space is enough.

First of all we need to ask ourselves, "Why is square footage important to me?" Is it because this is the commodity by which we generally set the value of real estate (i.e. price per square foot)? Is it a status symbol? Does having a bigger house help with my self-esteem? Do I need it for my kids to have enough space? Will I really miss that extra 3 to 10 inches along the exterior wall or would I rather be more comfortable? Is the floor space for keeping the things that I need? Do I really enjoy cleaning? Is all this space for the things that I want to accumulate?[38] Is it for housing my collection of DVDs or widgets? Wait a second…

Is a DVD collection something that you need when the world is going towards making everything smaller? A DVD collection is a great example because today, your DVD collection from 2003 can fit on a hard drive the size of 3 DVDs and access to nearly any movie at any time is now a reality by subscribing to Netflix or other streaming services from your cable provider. Take this a step further and consider how an iPad can now store an entire encyclopedia set that would have taken up several square feet of living space in the past while also being able to wirelessly receive and store any magazine you could possibly want. In fact, any tablet computer or eReader can now hold an entire library worth of books and fit into a backpack. *We are entering into a world of de-commoditization*. This is a good thing; since we are already exhausting the planets resources. Why buy more junk that will eventually end up in the landfill anyway while also reducing the amount of money that you have to live more fully? This is especially a great question to ask yourself if you are concerned about the initial cost of energy efficiency when planning your project. Floor space allows you to store more things while a better building envelope protects you, pays you back and reduces your dependence on a system that wants to keep you at work for the majority of your life.

In essence, we are living in a world where everything is getting smaller and having less clutter means living more fully.

Chapter 2

THE CONCEPTS THAT WILL HELP YOU SAVE ENERGY AND MONEY IN THE LONG TERM

THE IMPORTANCE OF R-VALUE OR INSULATION LEVEL

The R2000 standard, as previously mentioned, is a great measure by which to build a home. Unfortunately, while the R2000 standard addresses many of the key area's necessary to provide a comfortable and healthy environment, it does not adequately address the energy consumption of homes in the extreme prairie climate. In order to greatly reduce our energy usage and hence utility bills to get to net zero in a cold climate, we need to better prevent the usage of energy for heating (and cooling) by providing a better buffer (or R-value) between the indoors and the outdoors. To better understand this concept, investigate the image below to see how an average un-insulated basement appears to a thermal graphic (heat-sensing) camera.

Figure 1: Thermal graphic image of an un-insulated basement when outside air temperature (OAT) was reported as -10°C (though the ground and roof are still colder). Spot 1 is measured at -9.0°C in the image. This is slightly warmer than the OAT because the wall is heated slightly from the inside due to heat migration through the insulation. Spot 2 (the apparently un-insulated wall) is measured at -5.9°C is approximately 3°C warmer because it is heated from the warm air inside. This indicates that heat is transferred from the warmer basement to the colder outdoors more readily than through the upper walls due to the lack of insulation in the basement. Note that apparent temperatures shown in the windows are reflections of heat from the adjacent buildings.

In *Figure 1* you can see that the OAT has an effect on how easily heat is transferred from the inside to the outside. It is crucial to understand that while the un-insulated basement obviously transfers heat from the inside to the outside, even the insulated above grade wall is heated slightly via transferring heat from the inside to the outside because the exterior wall temperature is warmer than the outside air temperature.

The most important concept to understand in regards to why it's important to insulate better is the second law of thermal dynamics, which states that "two objects (or environments) that are at different temperatures will try to find equilibrium of temperature by transferring heat from the hot object to the cold object." This is best understood by observing that a hot cup of coffee will transfer its heat to the space until it reaches room temperature, or a cold drink will be heated by absorbing heat from a room until it reaches room temperature – that is, of course, unless they are stored in a well-insulated container.

Due to this law, though the home in Figure 1 is a couple yeas old, heat transfer occurs even on a relatively warm spring morning when the OAT is -10°C[39]. It is important to understand that *heat will always migrate from hot to cold; however, the rate at which it migrates is mostly determined by the R-value separating the two environments.*[40] Since it is so cold in the prairies, it becomes all the more important to prevent the heat from moving through the wall to the outside from the inside during the winter. It is also important to understand that the rate of heat transfer through an object increases as the difference in temperature between the two environments increases. As it gets colder outside, it gets colder inside faster. This is quite intuitive.

Thus, a house can be designed to have its walls, ceiling and floor insulated according to the average coldest climate that each surface experiences so that little to no energy input is required. Another way to understand this is that if the exterior wall temperature were to measure at the same temperature as the oat at a particular temperature, then very little heat migrates through the wall, hence the house should not require heating or cooling to keep the interior temperature from changing.[41]

This means that during the colder winter temperatures, heat transfer from the inside occurs more readily because the difference in temperature between the inside temperature (usually 22°C = 72°F) and the outside temperature increases (i.e. it gets colder outside). In scientific terms this is referred to as delta T (ΔT). If you are a scientific person and would like to understand this mathematically, the formula to understand R-value is $R=\Delta T/\dot{Q}_A$, where $\dot{Q}_A$ is the heat flux (heat transfer per unit area).

After many years of research, Dr. Rob Dumont suggests that in Saskatchewan we should be building houses with walls of approximately R50 to meet the demands of a prairie climate with minimal energy input.[42] In Canada most houses are currently built using 2x6 wall construction, which is filled with insulation batt that provides R20 within the wall cavity. However, *the actual R-value of a 2x6 wall is approximately R16 due to heat transfer through the studs* as is discussed and illustrated in the next section. With this in mind, it is no wonder that most houses in the prairies and in the far north would freeze in the winter without energy input within a few hours of losing electricity or gas.

While a larger buffer is generally better for both preventing heat loss in the winter and heat gain in the summer; there is a point where installing a wall system using too much insulation becomes more costly to install then the energy required to supplement the energy loss. This is where the code requirements for insulation have evolved from over time as energy prices have increased. As I have hopefully illustrated previously, energy prices will not be getting cheaper; hence, it is best to be prepared for these price increases by future proofing your investment when it is first built, rather than trying to improve your walls after the fact. Not only does this save you money on energy costs, but it greatly improves comfort within the home as well.[43]

I will show a couple more photos to illustrate a concept in simple terms.

The simplest way to reduce energy usage is to not require it at all. Increasing R-value prevents the transfer of heat energy from the interior to the exterior or vice versa. This prevents the need for energy input within the space, which is good for the environment.

Furthermore, if you live in a cold climate, are building a new home, and do not want to be dependent on a fossil fuel economy, this is the most cost-effective and efficient way to reduce your energy usage 24/7/365. While investing in technologies such as ground source heat pumps (commonly called geothermal), photovoltaic panels, wind turbines or solar thermal technologies for reducing your energy usage are great, these technologies are far less cost-effective then super-insulating by comparison.[44] Not only that, but super-insulating is a long-term investment that will continue to pay for itself for the life of your house, as there are no moving parts to wear out and maintenance should not be required if installed correctly.

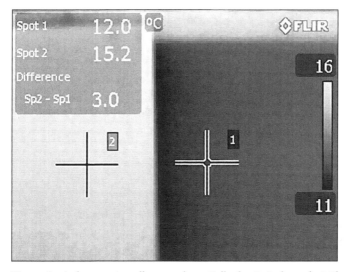

Figure 2: A basement wall covered partially by 2 inches of rigid "plastispan" R7.5 insulation.

The thermal graphic photo above shows a basement wall, which is insulated on the left side by a 2-inch-thick rigid insulation board (R7.5) on a bare concrete wall. The adjacent wall is connected to a garage, which has an interior temperature of approximately -4°C and is insulated on the garage side, making the actual heat transfer through the concrete much less than if the concrete were directly outside. The concrete wall is not insulated around the exterior and hence the entire wall is quite cool. The exposed piece of concrete in the photo on the right is actually a very small part of the wall. ***Notice that the left side of the insulated component prevents 3.1°C of heat transfer into the concrete wall.*** If this wall was completely uncovered, it would be a substantial energy drain when multiplied across the entire surface of the concrete wall. If that were the case, the cold concrete wall would continually be stealing energy from the warm interior and transferring that heat to the cold ground. This is a perfect example of why it is important to insulate a basement wall.

THERMAL BRIDGING IS BAD

As discussed above, the best way to reduce energy usage in a cold climate is to prevent heat transfer through the walls, ceiling and floor, as they are all assemblies in contact with the outdoors. With this in mind, remember that *not all materials are created equally in terms of how well or poorly they conduct heat.* This is evident if you have ever tried to pull a hot metal baking sheet out of the stove: the metal baking sheet conducts heat much better than the oven mitt that you are hopefully wearing. While this is evident in such an extreme example it also happens with the materials in your walls to a much less evident extent. Consider the thermal graphic images in Figure 3 that demonstrate how the 2x6 studs within the building assembly have a much lower R-value (about 1.25 per inch) compared to the R-value of the insulation within the walls (about 3.0 per inch for fiberglass).[45]

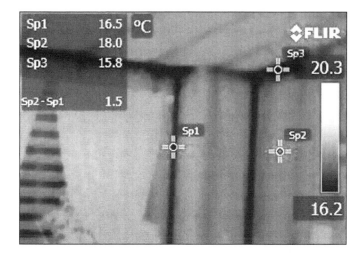

Figure 3: The top is a thermal graphic image providing an illustration of thermal bridging through a 2x6 stud wall. Darker shades correspond to cooler temperatures while white is the warmest. Exact measurements are shown in the top left of the photo. A temperature legend is on the right of the thermal graphic photo. The bottom image is an actual photo of the living space.

The images in Figure 3 were taken in the morning during an energy audit using a blower door to depressurize the house and accentuate air leakage. While no leakage is depicted in the photo, the figure demonstrates the heat transfer through studs in the wall of a regular 2x6 framed R20 wall house. This image was taken when the OAT was 5°C and interior temperature was 21°C. You can see that even during these relatively warm outside air temperatures, the interior wall is cooled by the outside to approximately 18°C. Such a temperature drop would not occur on a super-insulated wall. This temperature drop is most obvious where heat is transferred to the outside via the wood studs, which have a low R-value of approximately 6.5 through the width of the stud. This means that when it's colder outside, the transfer of heat occurs more easily and rapidly through the entire wall, though this is especially true through the studs. After seeing enough of these photos it becomes obvious that *thermal bridging is a significant source of heat loss through all building structures in cold climates*.

From the image above, you can see that even though the outside temperature is relatively warm, heat moves through the structural studs of the wall quite readily. This is the phenomenon that we want to prevent to the greatest extent possible both in the cold of the winter and heat of the summer. There are several methods of ensuring this, which are explained later, but the point is to ensure that the exterior wall is not in contact with an interior wall via materials that have low R-value.

Several techniques can be used to mitigate this problem and will be illustrated later in this book; however, the concept to understand is the same as the reason it is so important to insulate. We must prevent the extreme temperature on the exterior of the building from migrating to the interior. When it comes to minimizing thermal bridging, we must isolate the best conductors of heat between the two surfaces so that these conductors are not in physical contact with both the hot and cold side of the assembly. Ideally, we thermally isolate and prevent the exterior of the wall from being in contact with the interior wall. Doing so correctly not only prevents thermal bridging but also reduces the likelihood of cold spots that attract condensation and lead to areas of potential mold growth.

AIR LEAKAGE: OFTEN THE BIGGEST ENERGY WASTER

Air leakage is the result of penetrations in the building not being perfectly sealed or construction assemblies not fitting perfectly together due to the nature of the materials, quality of workmanship or shifting of the assembly over time. Air leakage typically occurs around doors, windows, vents, electrical boxes and places where building materials don't fit together properly. Often efficiency experts will demonstrate how to prevent air leakage by caulking or using spray foam around vents and windows. Doors and operational windows with leaks around the edges can usually be improved via the use of weather stripping.

Air leakage was traditionally of little concern and was even expected, as air leakage provided some ventilation to building occupants. Time and research have demonstrated, however, that air leakage can cause cold spots in wall cavities, which can lead to condensation collecting in these areas, particularly in cold climates. Over time, these areas of air leakage can become centers for mold to grow, which result in poor indoor air quality within the building and can even lead to the degradation of the wall itself. By some estimates, outside air leaking into the home, or air infiltration, is responsible for 40 percent of heating or cooling loss in the average home.[46]

Today, rather than allowing air to leak through parts of a wall unimpeded, we take measures to prevent air leakage by means such as wrapping the wall with a membrane, or filling in voids using spray foam. In doing so, we are:

- improving the efficiency of the wall and hence improving thermal comfort;
- preventing cold spots and hence potential condensation zones; and
- saving money on energy costs.

Note that if a once leaky house is sealed to become air tight, a means of providing mechanical ventilation such as a heat recovery ventilator (HRV) should be added to ensure that air changes occur regularly within the home (to be discussed later). Regular air changes will protect the health of occupants by removing contaminants such as VOCs and mold spores while also preventing air from becoming stagnant and creating respiratory problems. Insufficient air movement within a building not only smells bad, but it can also eventually cause mold growth and will literally rot the house from the inside out due to humidity accumulation. Insufficient ventilation was a problem when people first started building super-insulated houses and is likely the reason that high-efficiency envelopes didn't catch on with more gusto.

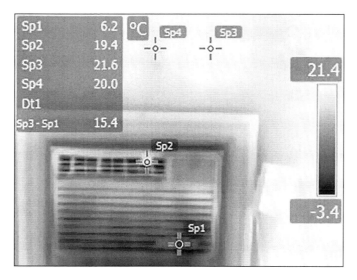

Figure 4: Cold air will also cool the space and transfer into the interior space via small air leaks. This figure demonstrates how a slight air infiltration around the air conditioner can cool an entire area demonstrated by Spot 1. Spot 3 demonstrates the temperature of the insulated portion of the wall. This situation demonstrates how a simple cover for your air conditioner can prevent much heat loss and improve comfort by preventing drafts.

THE IMPORTANCE OF A VAPOUR BARRIER

As mentioned previously, cold spots within a wall can be a breeding ground for mold. In a cold climate such as in Canada, this occurs primarily because warm moist air from the interior of a building comes into contact with a cold surface within a wall. If the warm moist air contains sufficient moisture or the surface is sufficiently cold, then the moisture within the air will condense on the cold surface. This phenomenon is readily observed when moisture accumulates on a mirror after a shower or when moisture gathers on a cold can of pop in a humid environment. To prevent the accumulation of moisture on a cold surface within a wall, the usage of a vapour barrier is required. *The importance of a continuous vapour barrier cannot be understated* with regards to protecting the long-term integrity of the wall.

The details regarding relative humidity (or humidity at a given temperature) are observable using a psychometric chart. Without demonstrating the use of a psychometric chart, one can still illustrate just how readily moisture can condense on a cold surface. Consider the average room at comfortable relative humidity. In most places this is in a typical room temperature situation where the room is at 22°C and a comfortable 50 percent relative humidity within the space. Under these conditions, moisture will condense on a surface that is colder than 12°C. If there is higher than 50 percent relative humidity within the room, such as after a shower or while cooking (100 percent relative humidity at a particular temperature is when fog within the air is visible), the temperature of the surface where water will condense will be higher than 12°C according to the relative humidity within the room. If the interior of a wall assembly becomes colder than 12°C due to migration of cold through the wall assembly (as a result of cold OATs or air leakage), then dryer air will condense on that surface. In areas with very cold OATs (such as in the Canadian prairies during the winter), air is likely to be very dry and hence moisture within the air will often dilute itself readily without coming into contact and condensing on an external wall. Problems are more likely to occur when the humidity levels within a home are high for long periods of time or when there is a lack of adequate ventilation. Specifics regarding calculations concerning relative humidity can be determined by learning how to use a psychometric chart.

So why is a vapour barrier important? Essentially, a vapour barrier is *a means of preventing the flow of moist air* from the hot side of a wall assembly to the cold side with the intent of preventing condensation on cold surfaces. There are many ways to create a vapour barrier. The most common and traditional method of creating a vapour barrier within a wall in Canada is by utilizing a 6 mil polyethylene plastic sheet, which is sealed and attached to the warm side of a wall assembly. The intent of this plastic is to provide a surface, which moisture cannot penetrate easily so that moisture from within the building will not migrate to inside the insulation cavity and condense on a cold wall during the colder months. During warmer months, moisture that finds its way into a wall cavity is expected to evaporate when the exterior wall is heated by the sun. However, this is not always the case.

A common polyethylene vapour barrier attached to the warm side of an exterior 2x6 wood framed wall.

Other methods of creating a vapour barrier include building the vapour barrier into the wall assembly itself. Such is the case with insulated concrete forms and structurally insulated panels. Additionally, spray foam insulation may be sprayed onto the interior side of an exterior wall or onto joists to provide both an air and moisture barrier while preventing the conduction of heat. If this layer of spray foam is sufficiently thick, it prevents the transfer of cold to the inside and hence a poly vapour barrier is not required. *Always check with local codes* with regard to the details of installing vapour barriers and other building components.

In some situations, rigid insulation is sealed on the exterior and provides a sufficient thermal barrier on the exterior of the wall assembly to prevent cold from the exterior from migrating to the interior. Depending on the width of the rigid insulation and on the local climate, this may also be accepted by some building codes as an acceptable vapour barrier.

It is important to note that creating two vapour barriers within the same wall assembly is typically not recommended as it can be very dangerous, particularly in a humid climate. This is because moisture that accumulates in the wall assembly during construction or moisture that gets trapped in the wall during the life of the building may become superheated during the summer months. If this moisture cannot migrate and be evaporated from the exterior, then it will find a way to migrate to the exterior and evaporate. There have been cases where such moisture has evaporated within a wall cavity, expanded and deteriorated the wall assembly causing the need for repairs.

THE SYSTEMS APPROACH TO ENSURING AN ENERGY-EFFICIENT BUILDING

As stated earlier, the best way to save energy in any building is to not require it in the first place. When it comes to space heating and cooling (the biggest usage of energy within a Canadian home), the best way to accomplish this is through sufficient insulation, which is used to prevent heat transfer from the hot side to the cold side. Heat is most readily transferred through air leaks in the walls or structure but is also readily transferred through the materials themselves. This concept is known as thermal bridging as was discussed above. To prevent thermal bridging, materials with a low R-value per unit of length (such as metal or wood studs) should not be in contact with both the cold side and warm side of a wall assembly.

This can be accomplished through several means, but all actively reduce the heat transfer or thermal bridging through the studs or other structural components while also increasing the R-value of the medium.

In other words, increasing R-value reduces the need for energy both in the winter and in the summer. By requiring less energy, equipment used for heating and cooling can be potentially sized smaller.[47] As a result, not only is less energy required to condition the space, but the equipment that is used to accomplish this can be much smaller and thus less costly during the initial installation. In other words, *the money that is spent on extra insulation is saved by using smaller equipment, making the cost of the project essentially the same*. The real savings, however, come via the reduced ongoing costs associated with energy required to operate the home or building.

A great example of this is a set of town houses in Regina on which Rob Dumont advised. Each rental unit was retrofitted to utilize a gas fireplace (cost $2,500) in the main open area of the unit and a thermostat controlled electric radiant heater (cost about $50 each) was added to each side room.[48] This was done to replace a full-scale furnace and ductwork install (cost approximately $10,000).

Other than saving approximately $7,000 on mechanical equipment and installation, an aesthetic feature was added to the house that uses less fuel and is required to operate less often. Additionally, better zone control within each room is achieved by having thermostatically controlled electric heat.

MAKE SURE THE INSULATION
IS CONTINUOUS

Before getting into building methods that reduce thermal bridging and air leakage while improving R-value, it's important to know that if an area is insufficiently insulated or a section is missing, then this area tends to act as a cold spot. If there are problems with the vapour barrier in the area of a cold spot, these areas tend to accumulate condensation as warm moist air will naturally migrate to these spots. As mentioned above, if this situation occurs within a wall, it is a breeding ground for mold, which is highly undesirable.

Such conditions are a potential health concern, especially for asthmatics and people with respiratory issues and allergies. It is essential to prevent this situation, as it has the potential to greatly affect the health of occupants while slowly degrading the house and making it lose value. In extreme cases, such homes can become dangerous to inhabit.

Chapter 3

Superior Building Methods

There are many ways to accomplish the same goal. In this case, the goal is reduced energy usage by reducing the need for space heating and cooling. As discussed earlier, the best way to reduce energy usage is not to require it at all. This is best accomplished by:

- improving the R-value of assemblies exposed to the outdoors (walls, ceilings and floors);

- reducing thermal bridging or the flow of heat through the materials used in construction; and

- controlling air movement into the building so that a healthy ventilation rate is achieved. Ventilation should be controlled in some manner so that it is accomplished efficiently and doesn't cause problems with the building assembly.

The information below is a summary that is meant to answer "what can I do to accomplish these goals?" I am not going to tell you how to build your home or what methods or materials you should use. This decision is up to you, as it will be made based on your climate, your goals, the expertise in your area and on what you are willing to pay for your home. I have listed the most common and cost-effective methods for meeting the goals above in an urban setting, as these options are generally accepted in all urban environments. In many jurisdictions, the use of the methods below is rewarded by local governments and utilities by providing grants and tax incentives to encourage the energy savings that these technologies create. Hence, once you understand this information, there is no real reason not to use these methods.

It is worth noting that there are many other "sustainable" building options that will not be described here such as straw bale, rammed earth, rail car, cobb or round wood due to the reluctance of municipal building regulators to allow these types of structures. However, I will likely blog about these options in the future or discuss them in a future publication.

Additionally, such a summary cannot possibly answer "how do I accomplish this?" for each and every situation. For this, you should consult a design and construction professional who is dedicated to providing the highest quality of workmanship to implement the techniques and install the products that will help you to achieve the levels of efficiency and quality as described in this book.[49] Such a directory is being created and accessible at: http://www.futureproofmybuilding.com/products_services/

These professionals will need to be aware of and take into consideration many complicated factors such as:

- your location and traditional climate;
- the size and shape of your building/lot;
- the orientation and details of your building/lot;
- the area exposed to the outside, i.e., walls, ceiling, floor;
- availability of labour, expertise and materials in your location; and
- your budget and preferences.

As with everything else, each building method has pros and cons and hence a summary of the method and pros and cons are listed below. Comparisons are generally based against standard wood frame construction (2x4 or 2x6 walls).

Disclaimer: I am not a contractor or architect and hence do not have sufficient experience with the methods listed below to tell you everything about them. Hence, there may be information regarding the methods below that is not complete or may not apply. I am relying on expert opinion via interviewing contractors and advisors, Internet and published research, and established knowledge to create the discussions and charts below. For this reason some contractors, vendors or other experts may disagree with the assessments below. In any case, if you understand the concepts of R-value, thermal bridging, air tightness and vapour barriers then you can make more informed decisions and I have accomplished my objective. I encourage you to conduct your own further research to determine the best method that will meet your needs and to read about all of the methods discussed prior to making a decision.

Note: it is essential to ensure that the wall assembly can breathe and therefore *the use of only one vapour barrier is recommended* for use within the wall assembly. If more than one vapour barrier is present, the potential exists for solar heat to vaporize any moisture trapped within the wall. This can potentially cause much damage to the wall. If two vapour barriers are used, this situation is more likely to occur in humid climates. In drier, colder climates (such as that of the Prairie Provinces) the goal for air tightness necessitating the need for two vapour barriers may outweigh the concern of solar heat vaporizing moisture trapped within a wall assembly.

DOUBLE WALL CONSTRUCTION

Double wall construction is a building method that utilizes two walls to thermally isolate the interior wall from the exterior wall. While more lumber is required in the construction of a double wall versus a single 2x6 wall, the distinctive advantage of double wall is that smaller dimension lumber (2x4 and 2x3) can be used at a reduced cost per unit from a standard 2x6 wall. Additionally, the blown-in cellulose, which is recommended is of lower cost than fiberglass batt or wall rock batt insulation.

As already demonstrated, having a separate wall that is not directly in contact with the outdoors is highly beneficial for reducing thermal bridging while also creating a customizable R-value for the finished wall. This can be accomplished by varying the distance between the two walls. The resulting cavity between the two walls will optimally be filled with blown-in cellulose (recycled newspaper combined with fire retardant) for the most cost-effective and high R-value per inch available, according to Dumont's research. However, this method does require expertise and is not yet widely implemented, as the conditions of our economy have not convinced people that such a high level of insulation is required.

If the application of blown-in insulation is not available individual walls can be spaced 3.5 inches apart and standard batt insulation would be used in between the stud wall assemblies. Individual batts would be laid vertically in the wall spacing, while batt insulation would be laid horizontally between the separate walls. If thinner walls are required, then a double wall can be implemented with two 2x4 framed walls assembled directly adjacent to each other (7.5 inches wide) with studs staggered so as to eliminate thermal bridging. In this way the wood studs are not in contact from exterior surface to interior surface.

There are many ways to utilize the double wall technique. Another method utilizes spray foam on the inside of the exterior wall to produce a superior air seal. In some jurisdictions, the use of 2 inches of spray foam on the interior wall (if installed by a certified professional) can substitute for a vapour barrier, which in many cases would greatly reduce the headache and labour associated with installing a formal poly vapour barrier.[50] If the code allows you to perform this option, it may be a time-efficient way to create a vapour barrier and save on labour costs at the expense of higher material costs for the spray foam.

The reason that double wall is listed first and discussed more extensively than the other methods is because double wall is the method that Rob Dumont has used to build his own house. This was the chosen method of construction by Dumont; after much research, the technology proved to be the most cost-effective, energy-efficient, customizable and environmentally friendly building option, particularly for an urban environment. Dumont has since used this technique in designs such as for the VerEco home to achieve high levels of thermal efficiency in an attempt to build the first Saskatchewan home to meet net zero. This technique is becoming more and more popular as many of the high-efficiency EQuilibrium homes utilize the double wall technique to achieve high levels of thermal efficiency.

For more information, details of how to build using the double wall technique are illustrated in the Canadian Home Builders Association Builders Manual in Chapter

11 (page 189). Dumont is the first listed "Technical Advisor" in this manual.

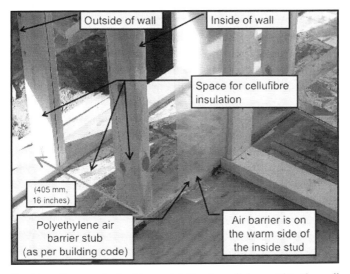

Double wall example sized to meet R60 using cellulose within the wall space. Original photo taken by Gordon Howel.[51]

Double Wall Construction Pros and Cons

Pros	Cons
Utilizes cheap, standard and readily available building materials: wood studs and cellulose (recycled newspaper with fire retardant), or batt insulation laid horizontally in the wall cavity.	Slightly increased labour component via construction and installation of an additional wall.
The building itself is a method of storing carbon for the life of the structure hence actively reducing climate change. This is particularly true if wood beams and cellulose are used rather than aluminum studs or rockwool.	Not widely implemented yet, so few contractors know how to do it well. Care must be taken to ensure that sufficient cellulose is added so that the cellulose doesn't settle and leave air gaps at the top of walls creating cold spots.
Conventional fiberglass batt or rock fibber insulation can be used instead of cellulose for ease of installation at increased cost.	Window sills require extra labour and expertise to install.
Relatively simple learning curve to implement.	Window sills may be a condensation zone if not properly sealed.
Large beautiful window sills.	Slightly reduced floor space within the dwelling due to thick walls if lot size is restricted.
Easily customizable during building for increasing the R-value of the structure as desired (simply build the walls further apart and use more cellulose). As illustrated above, R60 is achieved using 16 inches from exterior to interior.	If built off-site by a modular framing company, be aware that transporting the structure may be difficult and require extra care and attention from the staff that are moving it. This may introduce extra costs to the move.
Excellent sound buffer from the outside	Application of cellulose can be dusty.

Pros	Cons
Thermal bridging through studs is eliminated via two wall assemblies.	Cellulose must be kept dry during the construction process.
Walls can be built to several stories.	
Wood frame construction is advantageous in earthquake zones.	
With proper maintenance, wooden structures can last hundreds of years.	
Double wall can incorporate spray foam on the outer wall to provide superior air sealing and a more efficient vapour barrier. In some jurisdictions, 2 inches of spray foam can be used instead of poly vapour barrier if applied by a certified professional.	
Cellulose can be used in sound proofing interior walls, though it is more difficult to install than batt sound proofing.	

INSULATED CONCRETE FORMS

Insulating Concrete Form (ICF) is a system of formwork for concrete that are typically composed of various types of foam depending on the manufacturer. The forms resemble that of hollow Lego bricks which are interlocked and stacked together without mortar. The hollow interior of the stacked blocks is filled with concrete to provide structural strength. ICF are typically used for creating the structural walls or floors of a building. ICF construction is becoming increasingly commonplace for both low rise commercial and residential construction as more stringent energy efficiency and natural disaster resistant building codes are adopted.[52]

By its very nature, ICF construction eliminates thermal bridging by having a continuous layer of insulation both on the exterior and interior of the structural concrete. Because the blocks are all connected, ICF construction tends to be very air tight and has the bonus of not requiring a vapour barrier as it is already built into the system.[53] Additionally, it has a high thermal mass content due to the concrete used to provide structural strength though this thermal mass will have limited effect within the space during extreme cold conditions. In areas such as windows, this thermal mass will contribute to heat loss during winter if a sufficient thermal break is not incorporated. ICF construction is a great option in hot and humid climates, as the materials will not take on humidity and rot over time. ICF is also probably a better construction material than wood frame if a hot tub, steam room, yoga studio, gym or pool is to be placed inside the structure due to the humidity that these activites introduce in the space. Specially shaped ICF blocks are available for incorporating various architectural features into the building design. Also, extra insulation may be added to the exterior to improve the R-value performance of the wall assembly. This is a recommended practise in locations with extreme cold such as the Prairie Provinces.

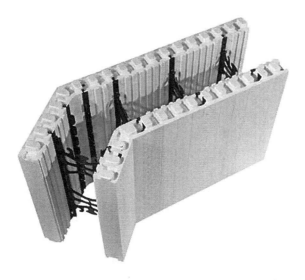

A common ICF block that demonstrates a 45 degree form.[54]

ICF Pros and Cons

Pros	Cons
Not highly labour intensive to assemble, but training and experience is required.	Costly to purchase the materials compared to conventional wood frame construction.
Walls are insulated on both the exterior and interior preventing moisture flow through the assembly.	Materials are typically made of foam products which are oil by-products. Soy-based polyurethane is available.[a]
By design, the assembly does not require a vapour barrier and is very air tight.	Foam "Lego like" blocks are filled with concrete. Concrete is made of 10 percent cement, which has a very high carbon foot print due to its manufacture and transportation.

Pros	Cons
ICF is an excellent option for basements or insulated crawl spaces due to thermal qualities and air tightness.	Limited R-value of R28 appears to be the maximum available for Logix platinum series. New code in Saskatchewan requires a minimum of R24 in walls thus the bare system is limited in its ability to provide higher R-value.[b]
A high thermal mass component prevents outdoor temperature swings from greatly influencing the interior of the building particularly in hotter climates, if the exterior is not a dark colour.	Proper installation requires that concrete must be tamped and walls must be braced properly during construction or the integrity of the walls is compromised.
Excellent sound buffer from the outside. Also useful for partitions between adjacent dwellings.	Like other oil-based products, the foam is probably quite toxic in the event of a fire; however, the building would likely still be standing.
Height restrictions allow for a multi-level home or low rise apartment building.	Installer must have sufficient experience to brace walls properly.
Different R-value wall systems are available (particularly in Europe), though these may be difficult to come by in North America.	Construction defects are difficult to identify even with a thermal imaging camera.
Works well for hot climates, as heat dissipates through the concrete into the ground if not thermally isolated at the slab.	Concrete has a low R-value. In cold climates concrete within the assembly must be thermally isolated from the slab and at the roof line to prevent heat loss through the assembly.
Running wires and pipes through the materials is relatively simple and can be covered by using spray foam.	Interior humidity in the first couple months after construction may be an issue as the concrete cures. This can and should be mitigated using dehumidification equipment.

Pros	Cons
Wind, water, mold, noise, drywall nail pop and earthquake resistant.[c]	
Cheaper insurance rates are offered in some jurisdictions due to structural and thermal benefits of ICF.	
Concrete and Styrofoam are a deterrent to rodents and insect pests compared to conventional wall systems (can be treated to prevent termites).	
ICF systems such as Nudura and Logix have a 4 hour fire rating.[d]	
Concrete cures within the form by retaining some of its moisture and hence has a tendency for high strength over time.	
Walls are very structurally strong. ICF homes are apparently able to handle tornados and even Hurricane Katrina.[e]	
The speed with which ICFs can be set, and the elimination of time spent stripping and cleaning forms, will usually offset the extra cost of ICFs, once the alternative insulation method is factored in.[f]	

a   Haefs, Brian. "Forms and Function". Green Building Solutions. American Chemistry Council, Inc.. Retrieved 2010-05-06.

b   Reverence Solplan Review January 2012 as taken from the proposed changes to the Canadian National Building Code.

c   http://thinkwithlogix.com/what.php

d   ICF facts and 4 hour fire rating – source http://thinkwithlogix.com/what.php

e   http://www.nbnnews.com/NBN/issues/2005-12-12/Building+Systems/index.html

f   http://www.proudgreenhome.com/blog/5852/Ask-the-Expert-Pros-and-cons-of-Insulated-Concrete-Form

FILL THE VOID WITH SPRAY FOAM

Spray foam insulation is an alternative to traditional building insulation in which two chemicals are combined to create expanding foam, which is sprayed against a surface (usually an interior wall) to provide a very air tight barrier of a high R-value.

There are two types of spray foam: open cell and closed cell. Closed cell spray foam is of very high R-value per inch of between R6 to R8 per inch at a cost of about $0.70 to $1 per board foot. The R-value of the finished foam barrier will depend both upon the type and brand used, as well as the thickness of foam applied. To avoid the potential for "burnout" or spontaneous combustion of the spray foam, closed cell spray foam must not be installed in passes greater than 2 inches thick, with time to allow the foam to cool before the next application is performed.[55] Closed cell foam is typically recommended for exterior usage because the air pockets are much smaller and provide a moisture barrier, as they do not absorb moisture as readily as open cell foam.[56] Open cell foam is hence better suited for interior applications such as for sound proofing. Open cell foam is about R3.6 per inch and costs approximately $0.44 to $0.65 per board foot.[57]

Open cell foam can be installed in thicknesses of up to 10 or 12 inches in a single pass.[58]

Open Cell spray foam installation. Notice its fluffy appearance.[59]

Closed Cell spray foam installation. The foam is denser than Open Cell which gives it a higher R-Value per inch.[60]

Though spray foam tends to be pricey, it has its benefits. Buildings treated with spray foam insulation insulate between 30 percent and 50 percent, better than traditional wood frame and batt insulation.[61] In addition to a continuous and space filling thermal barrier, spray foam insulation that is sprayed in buildings protects against moisture by reducing cold spots and air infiltration. This provides the benefit of reducing the chance of harmful mold and mildew from growing within the structure while also preventing pollen and spores from the outside from entering through leaky areas.[62] As mentioned earlier, eliminating mold growth reduces the likelihood of rotting wood in a home and the likelihood of allergic reactions to mold spores.

In addition to building temperature and moisture control, spray foam insulation is also useful for reducing noise (though it is often more expensive than cellulose, rockwool or fiberglass sound dampening technologies). When properly applied, foam insulation serves as a barrier to airborne sounds and reduces airborne sound transfer through a building's roof, floor and walls.

Spray foam has a distinct advantage in that it can be applied to almost any surface and will expand to fill existing cavities to prevent heat and air movement. Spray foam can be sprayed onto roof tiles, concrete slabs, into wall cavities, or through holes drilled into a cavity of a finished wall (in small amounts). Spray foam is also very beneficial for reducing the effects of thermal bridging by coating beams and other structural members that are in direct contact with the exterior of a building. It is advisable to *apply spray foam to the floor and ceiling trusses around the exterior of the building*, as this typically is an area of high thermal bridging.

As mentioned earlier in the double wall section, a 2-inch coating of spray foam can be applied to the interior side of an exterior wall to provide approximately an R14 thermal barrier to the wall. If applied by a certified installer, then this can be used instead of a formal vapour barrier. However, as always, confirm this with your local codes.

The problems with spray foam typically come from the fact that the area to which it is applied requires very good ventilation while it is being applied and while it is curing. The application process is often very messy; therefore, careful preparation before installing spray foam in existing buildings is necessary. Additionally, the chemical components used in large-scale applications of spray foam have to be heated to a specific temperature to cure and adhere correctly.

Spray Foam Pros and Cons[63]

Pros	Cons
Can be applied to many surface types to create an air tight thermal barrier of varying R-value according to foam thickness.	Cost tends to be quite high for material and installation. Most sellers sell by "inches applied per square foot."
Can be implemented in very difficult locations.	Application is toxic in nature and must be done with proper safety equipment or by a trained professional.
Due to its ability to conform to spaces, spray foam is excellent for reducing thermal bridging.	Improper installation through bad mixing of components can result in poor insulation and curing.

Pros	Cons
Some spray foams are derived from plant-based oils, which are a renewable resource. Choose these ones where possible.	Traditionally, spray foams were derived from petroleum products. Many are now derived from plant products such as soy and castor beans.
Excellent option for improving existing walls.	Spray foam releases VOCs while being installed and while curing; thus, ventilation of the area in which it was applied must be very good to prevent remnant odours.
The addition of foam improves the sound buffer from the outside.	Spray foam contents must be heated to the proper temperature to be applied correctly.
Spray Foam Insulation does not cause itching when touched.	Most inspectors require spray foam to be covered with an approved thermal barrier such as 1/2-in. drywall.
It prevents the entry of bugs into the home and can therefore save on extermination bills in areas where this is a problem.	Spray Foam emits toxic fumes containing isocyanides when burnt. The harmful fumes badly affect the lungs.
Spray foam can be applied to existing walls in specific ways to improve the R-value of the walls.	Spray Foam Insulation needs to be protected from harsh sunlight and chemical solvents.
Spray Foam Insulation is used to decrease noise and sound radiation through a building's floor, roof and walls.	R-value of a Spray Foam Insulation decreases with age.
Some codes allow for the application of spray foam to a thickness of 2 inches or R14, which removes the need for a conventional poly vapour barrier.	Spray foam makes a huge mess when installed. Remove all tools and all personnel that don't need to be there. Be prepared for a potentially time-consuming clean-up.
Over time the application of spray foam hardens the wall assembly that it is applied to.[64]	Be aware of the potential for spontaneous combustion of the spray foam product. Recommend using a certified installer.

RIGID INSULATION

Rigid insulation is essentially hard foam that comes in sheets. Sheets can be made of several different materials to produce varying R-value per inch. Sheet boards also come in varying thicknesses to accommodate space issues.

One type of rigid foam board insulation shown here in 2 inch thick sheets. Rigid insulation comes in varying sizes and several widths of varying R-values as determined by the material of which it is composed.

For those that insist on building a traditional single wall wood frame construction, rigid insulation around the exterior of a building is an excellent way to improve the air barrier of the building while also greatly reducing the incidence of thermal bridging through studs by providing a continuous thermal barrier around the building. Some types of rigid insulation can even act as a moisture barrier and structurally insulated sheathing.[65] In various applications, different types of rigid can also be used in the interior to improve the R-value of the wall assembly. The use of strapping is usually required when working with rigid to provide both an air space and a surface on which to mount finishing.

Rigid insulation (installed around the exterior of a concrete basement while the building is constructed) is often *a cost-effective way of reducing energy usage and ensuring thermal comfort within the basement*. It is important to note that when rigid insulation is applied to the exterior, it should be sealed from moisture using "blue skin" or some other type of peal and stick non-permeable membrane to prevent water vapour from deteriorating the foam. It drives me crazy to see how many basements aren't being insulated from the outside during construction, even though it is very quick, cheap and relatively easy to accomplish while the building is being constructed. Typically, the insulation can simply be glued against the concrete wall before the area around the foundation is filled. The filled dirt holds the insulation in place and now moist and cold dirt does not directly contact the very low R-value concrete foundation wall. An example of this would be to use 2 -inch-thick layer of closed cell rigid against the foundation at a cost of approximately $25 for a 4x8 piece, providing an approximate R-value of 7.5 against the exterior of the concrete. Hence the cost to thermally isolate the basement of a standard home is approximately $1,100 in material costs with the cost of blue skin factored in. But the benefits don't end there.

Insulating the outside of the basement works well with damp-proofing and foundation drainage. Rigid fiberglass[66] can act as a drainage layer, keeping surface and ground water away from the foundation. Adding insulation from the exterior helps keep walls at room temperature, which protects the structure by reducing the risk of interior condensation while increasing comfort in the basement. If insulation is not added to the exterior of the basement wall, then the concrete walls are in direct contact with the dirt, making them the same temperature as the ground (approximately 4°C in most areas of Saskatchewan). This turns the wall into a condensation zone and hence potential mold hotspot, if a proper vapour barrier is not installed. The only real disadvantage to insulating the foundation during construction, other than a slight cost, is that the insulation needs to be covered above grade, which may add a slight amount of labour.

Rigid insulation can also be used on the interior of a concrete wall to provide a quick and easy vapour barrier/ thermal barrier if sealed properly with tuck tape. As always, check with your local codes as this may or may not meet with the building inspectors expectations of a suitable vapour barrier.

Rigid Insulation Pros and Cons

Pros	Cons
Utilizes cheap, standard and readily available building materials: wood studs as per standard construction with added rigid Styrofoam on the interior or exterior.	Slightly increased labour component via installation of the rigid and bracing for siding or drywall.
Likely the cheapest method to reduce thermal bridging particularly with existing walls.	Must consult with local building codes to determine the best way to implement.
Simple learning curve to implement.	Rigid insulation is typically derived from oil.

Pros	Cons
Different R-values and hence wall thicknesses are created by different combinations of framed wall plus thickness and R-value of rigid foam insulation.	Window sills may require extra labour and expertise to install.
The addition of foam improves the sound buffer from the outside.	Rigid insulation is somewhat delicate and must be handled carefully.
Rigid foam can be added to both the interior and exterior to greatly increase the R-value.	Moisture control is important to prevent the rigid from allowing moisture to pass through it and deteriorate unventilated material.
The effects of thermal bridging through studs are greatly reduced, and hence heat transfer through the wall is greatly reduced where rigid is used properly.	Rigid insulation will degrade if exposed to the sun for long periods.
Rigid foam can be added to an existing wall in an already constructed house.	Strapping through the rigid will be necessary for hanging drywall when rigid is applied on the interior wall over studs.
Does not reduce floor space as much as double wall, especially if rigid is applied to the exterior.	
Easily implemented under slabs and on basement floors.	
If applied along the basement wall during construction, an effective moisture barrier is created while also keeping the basement wall warmer. This reduces the potential for moisture problems in the basement.[67]	

USE ALUMINUM TO REFLECT HEAT TO WHERE YOU WANT IT

Additional efficiency can be attained using a reflective aluminum surface on either the rigid insulation, or on the vapour barrier itself. This is because aluminum foil has a high reflectivity of between 86 percent and 98 percent in the infrared ranges of indoor temperature.[68] This means that infrared radiation (or heat) from within the building will hit the reflective aluminum surface and reflect back into the space. In order for this to be effective, an airspace of at least 3/4 of an inch between the aluminum surface and the closest surface to the space (usually drywall) is required. Since the heat is reflected to sit in between the reflective insulated surface and drywall within a thin air layer, it is difficult to assess the exact benefit this has concerning retaining heat within a space. Additionally, since the reflection of heat is difficult to measure precisely, the reflected heat may not be reflected directly back into the space. Reflected heat is not directly related to the R-value of a material, thus the jury is still out on how effective this is in colder climates for keeping interior spaces warm. This effectiveness is particularly difficult to determine because the reflected heat is likely to stay trapped between the drywall and reflective barrier.

Rigid insulation covered with a layer of thermally reflective foil.

Cost will likely be an issue when installing aluminum vapour barrier or aluminum coated rigid insulation as it is slightly more expensive than standard rigid. If rigid insulation coated in aluminum is used on the interior of a wood frame building, this situation is likely to provide an excellent thermal break and reduce thermal bridging through the studs while also reflecting a significant proportion of the heat back into the space. The precise benefits to the thermal performance by building using this technique are still being experimented with and modeled.

In hot climates, aluminum reflective surfaces are commonly used on the exterior side of the insulation component of buildings in areas such as roofs, or exterior walls to reflect the suns heat away from the building's interior. This is a cost–effective strategy that prevents the migration of heat to the interior and hence saves energy by mitigating the need for cooling. Several options exist for implementing thermally reflective insulation as it is available in rolls of various dimensions.

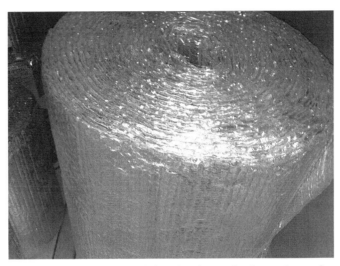

A roll of thermally reflective foil used to line walls, ductwork or ceiling spaces. Commonly and more effectively used in hot climates. Do not rely on this to prevent the migration of heat in extreme cold.

STRUCTURAL INSULATED PANELS (SIPS)[69]

Structural insulated panels (or structural insulating panels), SIPs, consist of an insulating layer of rigid polymer foam sandwiched between two layers of structural board. The structural board can be sheet metal, plywood, cement or oriented strand board (OSB) and the foam either expanded polystyrene foam (EPS), extruded polystyrene foam (XPS) or polyurethane foam.

SIPs put the insulation on the inside of the member as opposed to ICF which have insulation on the outside. In this depiction the structural board is plywood.[70]

SIPs can be used as the structural members in a building and share the same structural properties as an I-beam or I-column. The rigid insulation core of the SIP acts as a web, while the OSB sheathing exhibits the same properties as the flanges. SIPs combine several components of conventional buildings, such as studs and joists, insulation, vapour barrier and air barrier into a solid piece. They can be used for many different applications, such as exterior wall, roof, floor and foundation systems. Depending on the materials used to comprise the structural board, SIPs can be very structurally strong. Additionally, they can be manufactured and assembled into a finished, light-weight product in a single location. It is for these reasons that SIPs are becoming increasingly more popular in modular housing design.

SIPs work as framing, insulation and exterior sheathing, and can come precut from the factory for the specific job; hence, the exterior building envelope can be built quickly. SIPs have the distinct advantage that the assembly itself is a solid unit, which is designed and built to eliminate thermal bridging and when placed together properly will be air tight. Additionally, the labour component associated with assembling SIP buildings is less than with a traditional framed building. The use of a crane may be necessary, though, and panels may be damaged in transport if proper care and attention is not taken.

Different manufacturers will have different products with varying effectiveness and cost. Panels typically come in widths ranging from 4 to 12 inches thick. A standard 4-inch-thick panel typically achieves R13.8 with minimal thermal bridging due to its construction properties.[71] A table for R-value Comparison to Fiberglass is listed below from a separate source, though it is difficult to say how accurate this is. It is recommended that the minimum panel of 6 inches be used for the Canadian climate. Note that the thicker the SIP used, the more money the panel will likely cost.

R-value Comparison of SIPS to Fiberglass:[72]

Panel Thickness	Actual R-value	Performance Value
4 ½"	R-17	R-25
6 ½"	R-25	R-38
8 ¼"	R-33	R-50
10 ¼"	R-41	R-62
12 ¼"	R-48	R-72

SIPS Pros and Cons

Pros	Cons
Not highly labour intensive due to the completed structure of the panels. Fewer tradespeople will be required for installation, reducing labour costs if a crane is not required.	Costly to purchase the materials compared to standard wood framing. Transportation costs may also be an issue.
Panels can be used as floor, wall and roof, with the use of the panels as floors being of particular benefit when used above an un-insulated space below.	Materials are made of Styrofoam, which is an oil by-product, though biologically-based alternatives exist.
Continuous insulation within the assembly has been shown to outperform a standard 2x4 wood frame wall with fiberglass batt.	Depending on panel size used, a crane may be necessary for installation; hence, site restrictions may be an issue.
Does not require a vapour barrier and is very air tight if installed properly.	Requires a flat foundation to ensure proper installation. Panels must be fitted together correctly to prevent air leakage and drafts.
High axial load strength.	Availability of materials may be an issue.
Multiple sizes and material types are available for multiple applications. These include metal as the structural board component.	
Height restrictions may be an issue for certain types of panel.	

R-VALUE CHART OF COMMON INSULATING MATERIALS

A detailed description of the R-values of wall assemblies is displayed here for easy reference. This table has been taken from the website:
cmhc-schl.gc.ca/en/co/maho/enefcosa/enefcosa_002.cfm

Insulation Material	R/in. (RSI/m)	Appearance	Advantages/ Disadvantages
Batt-Type			
Fibreglass	3.0 – 3.7 (21 – 26)	All batts come in plastic-wrapped bales. The products are like fibrous blankets, about 1.2 m (48 in.) long and wide enough to fit snugly between wall studs.	Readily available.
Mineral wool	2.8 – 3.7 (19 – 26)	Same as Fibreglass.	Somewhat better fire resistance and soundproofing qualities than Fibreglass.
Cotton	3.0 – 3.7 (21 – 26)		Not readily available.
Loose-Fill All loose-fill insulations typically require a professional installer.			
Fiberglass	3.0 – 3.7 (21 – 26)	A very light fibrous fill, usually pink or yellow.	Can be affected by air movement in attics.
Mineral fibre	2.8 – 3.7 (19 – 26)	A very light fibrous fill, usually brown.	

Insulation Material	R/in. (RSI/m)	Appearance	Advantages/ Disadvantages
Cellulose fibre	3.0 – 3.7 (21 – 26)	Fine particles usually grey in colour, denser than glass or mineral fibre.	Provides more resistance to air movement than other loose-fill insulations. Can have settlement problems if not installed properly.
Board-Stock			
Type I and II (expanded) polystyrene or EPS	3.6 – 4.4 (25 – 31)	White board of small — about 8 mm (0.3 in.) in diameter — foam beads pressed together.	Typically HCs used in production. Must be covered.
Type III and IV (extruded) polystyrene or XPS	4.5 – 5.0 (31 – 35)	Commonly blue or pink foam board.	Works well in wet conditions, can act as a vapour retarder. HFC usually used in production. Must be covered.
Rigid fibreglass	4.2 – 4.5 (29 – 31)	A dense mat of fibres, typically less rigid than polystyrene.	Drains water away. Sometimes hard to find.
Rigid mineral fibre	4.2 – 4.5 (29 – 31)	See "Rigid fibreglass" above.	Drains water away.
Polyisocyanurate	5.6 – 6.7 (39 – 46)	Foil-faced rigid foam.	HFC usually used in production.
Spray-Applied All spray-applied insulations fill cavities very well. They must be applied by a specialized contractor.			
Wet-spray cellulose	3.0 – 3.7 (21 – 26)	Fine particles held in place by a binder.	

Insulation Material	R/in. (RSI/m)	Appearance	Advantages/ Disadvantages
Open -cell light density polyurethane	3.6 (25)	A soft, compressible spray foam that expands into the cavity.	Can act as the air barrier if combined with another material. Must be covered with a vapour barrier.
Closed cell medium density polyurethane	5.5 – 6.0 (38 – 42)	A rigid spray foam that expands into the cavity and sets up fairly rigid.	Can act as the air barrier and vapour retarder. HFC used in production. Must be covered.

Note: All values are approximate and for general comparison only. Some insulations may be irritants or hazardous during installation. Consult manufacturers' recommendations and insulation packaging for proper respiratory, eye and skin protection.

You can also consult the link below for another account of the R-value of materials:
en.wikipedia.org/wiki/Building_insulation_materials

The bottom line: Increase the R-value of all surfaces that are in contact with the outdoors. Ideally, thermal bridging of materials exposed to the outdoors should be minimized via the wall assembly by means of preventing low R-value components (i.e., studs, metal beams or concrete components) from direct contact with the outdoors and indoors. Ensure that the facility is airtight to prevent energy loss. In extreme climates, use mechanical ventilation in super-insulated or air tight buildings to ensure that sufficient airflow is present to prevent mold growth.

Chapter 4

More Important Things
to Understand

WINDOWS CAN BE AN ENERGY PROBLEM
OR AN ENERGY SOLUTION

Windows are wonderful. Unless you are a vampire, you probably love natural light. Natural light makes us feel good and its usage in internal spaces is an essential component of a good design. With that in mind, there is obviously a trade-off between windows and efficiency, and hence it should be of little surprise that *windows are the main source of heat gain in hot months and one of the main sources of energy loss in buildings in colder months*, especially if they are over used within the building. This is because even the highest quality triple pane windows have a very low thermal resistance of R6.6 (U=0.15).[73] This means that if you are spending money to build walls that meet R30 or R50 to reduce your energy usage, it makes sense that you want to reduce the wall space where the best thermal resistance you can achieve is R6.6. Not only that, but when you consider that windows are quite costly per unit area compared to walls, it makes sense from a financial point of view to be strategic when sizing and placing windows.

Windows are a complicated subject, so without getting too much into the optimal usage of windows right now, it is important to know that if planned well and orientated correctly, windows can be the source of what is called Passive Solar Heating. Buildings designed with passive solar in mind can greatly reduce the heating load necessary in the winter while remaining cool and comfortable in the summer. Essentially, this means that if windows are sized and correctly placed, not only do they provide a great source of light, but they also save a significant amount on energy bills in both winter and summer. How much exactly? Well, according to the Canadian Home Builders Association Building Manual, between 15 percent and 40 percent of your space heating requirements can be met by the sun during the winter for free. If correct shading is incorporated into the design, these windows are also shaded correctly in the summer and hence your house will stay cool for free.[74] Both of these conditions are provided if the window placements on the north, east and west sides of the structure are appropriately sized. If you are looking to build with passive solar heating, first calculate the floor area of the building. A good rule of thumb is to have between 6 percent and 10 percent of glass area on the south wall and no more than 4 percent glass on the north wall, in comparison to the square footage of the house.[75]

To understand this concept, consult Figures 5 and 6. Basically, in the northern hemisphere (north of the tropic of Cancer) the sun will always be in the south traveling from east to west and will be at its maximum height or due south at solar noon (this is how noon is determined for a given time zone). With the proper sized overhang, the correct building orientation (long side running east to west—design it this way if possible) and substantially more windows on the south side, a building will capture a great deal of heat in the winter and keep it out in the summer, while still having a nice source of light year round.

A great and handy resource for understanding and calculating window sizes, shading, building orientation and solar gains can be found at: http://susdesign.com/tools.php.

If you use these tools, please support the developer, as indicated on the web page. It would take considerable effort to create these tools and they are posted free of charge on the website.

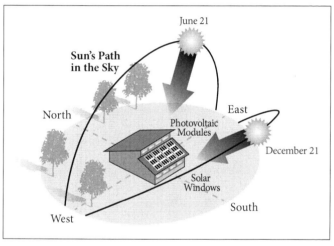

Figure 5: An illustration of the sun's path through the sky in the northern hemisphere. Notice how the hot summer sun is shaded by the roof and the winter sun is allowed to enter the building via windows to provide heat. Note: If you live in the southern hemisphere, the sun will always be somewhere in the north.[76]

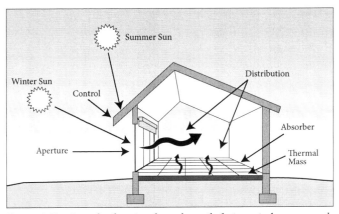

Figure 6: Passive solar heating through south-facing windows, properly sized shading and thermal mass.[77]

Window Tips: Don't use aluminum windows unless they are used as an interior window to thermally protect an external double or triple pane window. Aluminum frame sliding windows are very inefficient. The best and hence most expensive are triple-glazed with two low e-coatings, argon-gas-filled. This type of window was used on the VerEco home to get maximum R-value for the entire building. On the south side, use windows with a high solar heat gain factor (SHGF) > 0.55. Design the building to have a higher R value on the north, east and west by having modest-sized windows but be sure that they are sufficiently large so that they meet the fire codes. Windows should have R5 or greater. Solar heat gain is not as important for these windows so SHGF should be lower than .55 especially on the east and west sides in hotter climates. Use the lowest SHGF windows you can afford on the east and west in hot climates as this will greatly reduce the need for air conditioning.

If project cost is an issue, spend more money on the envelope of the building to get a higher R value wall system and use double-pane windows instead of triple pane. Your project will have a much higher efficiency that way.

Other methods of conserving heating or cooling energy within a home include using thermal mass to store the energy or using thermally reflective materials within the walls, as was discussed in the rigid insulation section.

EVERY EXTERIOR SURFACE IS A SOURCE OF ENERGY LOSS IN WINTER

With all of this discussion of increasing the R value of surfaces that are in contact with the outside, it stands to reason that an easy way to reduce energy usage is to reduce the surface area in contact with the outside. With that in mind, the shortest distance between two points is that formed by a straight line. Consequently, building a straight wall is typically much easier and hence cheaper than a wall with unnecessary protrusions which are created for features such as closets, fancy roof lines etc. I am not suggesting that we should all have perfect rectangles for each building, as that would be boring and largely unappealing. This is one of the trade-offs that design professionals make regularly that affect the dynamics of the entire building.

Without getting into the debate of what is architecturally and aesthetically appealing, it stands to reason that there are inherent compromises between that which is efficient and that which is pretty. Be aware of this during the design phase of your new home.

RAISE THE ROOF

Since heat rises, the roof is where the majority of the heat loss is likely to occur. Hence, the ceiling is the area that must be the best insulated surface to trap that heat in. In doing so, the heat required during the winter stays within the structure much better.

Having a well-insulated ceiling is also highly beneficial in the summer. Since the majority of roofs are covered in black shingles, during the summer months, the roof space tends to absorb much solar radiation and can get quite hot. By having a well-vented roof along with a high R value ceiling, the transfer of heat from the roof is greatly impeded, resulting in a lower need for air conditioning during the summer (if any at all).

To achieve a high efficiency within your roof, it is advisable to build the roof with raised trusses in order to accommodate *at least 2 feet (24 inches) of blown-in fiberglass or cellulose*. this will provide approximately R60 in the ceiling space.

THE IMPORTANCE OF VENTILATION

Ventilation requires energy. This is especially true in extreme climates because either extremely cold air must be heated or very hot and/or humid air must be cooled and dehumidified. Thus, there is an inherent trade-off between a healthy level of ventilation and energy efficiency.

Insufficient ventilation (airflow) is often the result when leaky areas of an existing building are sealed or when a building is super-insulated without having proper mechanical ventilation. Insufficient fresh air entering a space contributes to lingering odours, musty smells and even to the fatigue and poor health of occupants. Poor ventilation is not only unpleasant for occupants, but eventually it can cause breathing problems and mold issues, which can affect the integrity of the building. For this reason, it is essential to have sufficient ventilation to manage odours and provide fresh air without over ventilating and hence reducing efficiency. A good rule of thumb, as suggested by Energuide, requires 0.3 air changes per hour (ACH) for the average modest-sized home as being a suitable minimum level for health and comfort. This minimum level of 0.3 ACH is suitable for about four occupants, depending on the overall size of the house. If there are more occupants or excessive condensation is noticed on windows regularly, then a higher rate of ventilation is likely required.

For many older homes, windows and leaks within the structure are the primary sources of ventilation. Given that in most of Canada the usage of windows in the winter time is not advisable for producing cross-ventilation, the installation of a Heat Recovery Ventilator (HRV) is recommended, though not required, by the National Building Code of Canada.[78] Fortunately, some local jurisdictions are beginning to mandate the installation of HRVs to ensure proper ventilation in new buildings.

A heat recovery ventilator is basically a device that removes heat from warm indoor air as it is being exhausted from bathrooms and kitchens[79] and transfers that heat to the cold incoming air from the outdoors without mixing the two air streams together. The heat that is removed from the exhaust air is energy that was already paid for and is being reused to prevent the need for as much heating of cold outside air used in ventilation. These systems are very effective at providing adequate ventilation while also reducing the need to burn extra fuel in order to supply the space with fresh air. The effectiveness or efficiency of the unit is related to the size of the collectors and is a function of the difference in the outdoor air temperature and indoor air temperature.

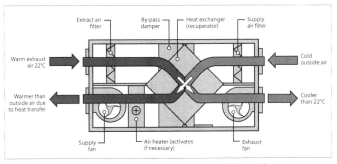

An illustration of the basic operation of an HRV with approximate temperatures.

THERMAL MASS WITHIN THE STRUCTURE

Gaining weight is not something that most people like to think about, but it's a great idea within a well-designed building. As noted earlier, thermal mass is important for controlling the heat gain through windows in passive solar design because the mass is heated throughout the day. By having a strategic thermal mass in place to capture the heat from sunlight, fast temperature swings within the space are minimized and maximum heat is captured when it is available. This heat is then stored in the mass for use at night or when the temperature begins to drop. Since it takes time both for a mass to heat as well as to cool, heating or cooling in this manner is most effective in open floor plans.

Heating or cooling of a mass requires more energy than air and hence takes much longer if the heating is done via passive solar. This is why temperature spikes within a building can be better regulated by using thermal mass in passive solar design; rather than overheating the air once sufficient sunlight has heated the interior, the excess heat is then absorbed by the mass. What happens is that once a body captures heat, it will also radiate it out slowly until temperature equilibrium occurs with the surfaces with which the mass is in contact. This phenomenon is essentially a description of the second law of thermal dynamics.

Thermal mass can also be understood in terms of cooling. This can best be understood using the analogy of a refrigerator. The reason that it is more efficient to leave a fridge full than empty is because, once the contents within the fridge are brought to temperature, an inrush of warm air comes in every time the fridge is opened. By having the fridge full of cans (for example) creates a thermal mass within the fridge and reduces the fridges need to cool as much air every time the door opens, because there is less air, and the cans participate in the cooling of the air. Though energy is required to initially bring the mass (cans) down to the temperature within the fridge, less energy is required to keep the mass cool than to continually cool the air that floods the fridge.

HOW TO ADD THERMAL MASS
COST–EFFECTIVELY

There are several ways to add thermal mass to a structure, all with varying costs and applications. The easiest ways are typically making walls and floors of concrete, stone or tile. Some designers will even advocate storing excess drywall scraps or other dense non-flammable, non-decaying materials in the interior walls to add thermal mass to the structure. This has the benefit of using scrap material and hence preventing it from ending up in a landfill. Depending on the material added to the walls, it may be possible to add loose-fill cellulose or spray foam to the wall to add a level of sound proofing, or just put sound proofing in the walls.

Partition walls, countertops and kitchen islands that are made of stone or concrete are also great methods for adding aesthetic thermal mass to a space, *provided that proper structural support for these items exists and was designed into the structure*. An example of this would be to strategically place a kitchen island made of concrete in an area that is directly heated via passive solar. In doing so, more energy can be captured and stored during the heat of the day and released during the night.

Radiant floor heating is also a means of creating thermal mass within the floor. Since water weighs significantly more than air, it works much better as a heating or cooling medium than air. This is why boilers and radiant systems are far more efficient than air systems. The downside to using thermal mass in an application such as a hot water radiant heating is that water systems have a slow response time and hence are more difficult to control, particularly during the spring and fall. Because of this people tend to further complicate the situation because they tend to turn up the thermostat to compensate for the slow response time and hence overheat the space. Another drawback is that in-floor radiant systems are expensive to install and tend to be overkill in super-insulated houses, especially ones with an insulated slab. This is not an argument against the merits of in-floor heating, but rather one of balancing costs. It comes down to a balance of priorities as well. People tend to like radiant heating better because their bodies feel the heat directly as opposed to feeling heated air. As a building becomes larger, the benefits and paybacks of in-floor heating increase.

SHADING IS COOL

While the majority of this book is about reducing the amount of heat needed within a space, cooling in most parts of the world is the primary usage of energy.[80] As with heating, the best way to save energy on cooling costs is to not require cooling at all. In any climate a super-insulated house will have a low rate of heat gain if the windows are properly shaded. This is because windows can gain approximately 200 BTU per square foot per hour if un-shaded. The best way to shade against heat gains within a space is from the outside. This can be accomplished by purchasing windows with low emissivity (Low E) coatings or by incorporating overhangs or exterior shades into the building. These solutions can sometimes be logistically difficult to incorporate after the building is constructed; however curtains and roller shutters of various shades can also be used inside a space to provide a reduced heat gain to the interior. Window coatings can also used to reflect the suns rays rather than allow them to pass through the glass into the space. Window coatings can be added to existing windows and are a low cost solution on the east and west sides of a building. They can also be used on south facing windows that are not properly shaded for passive solar gains.

The best long term way to shade a house from the outside is to strategically use nature's air-cleaning, soil-holding oasis makers: that is, trees. By planting deciduous trees (leafy) on the east and west side of a structure the heat load added to the structure during the summer can be minimized on walls, windows and eventually large sections of the roof. This is best done on the east and west to not only provide shading but to keep solar access available on the south side of the building. The extent of the effectiveness of this shading is dependent on many factors such as the height of the structure, the age and type of tree as well as the foliage of the tree. A bonus of using deciduous trees is that the leaves fall off and allow light to strike the structure during the late fall and winter months which will have a heating effect when it is desired. By planting evergreen trees on the east and west shading is provided year round. When deciding where and what types of trees to plant, be courteous and careful not to shade or steal the sunshine from your neighbour, who may one day want to harvest solar energy for producing electricity or hot water. Also make sure not to plant them too close to the foundation of your home as the tree roots may one day give you problems.

In large open areas, it is also a good idea to plant evergreen trees on the north side of a structure to provide maximum protection from the wind in the winter, as they do not lose their foliage. Having a sufficient wind break in the north can greatly reduce the heat loss during colder months and save significant energy in windy areas .

Bottom Line: If you are in a building that is constantly overheating in the summer, a cheap and aesthetic long term solution is to plant trees near the structure on the east and west sides to shade it. In the short term utilize window coatings, blinds or roller shades in the short term or when trees are not permissible.

THE FUTURE OF LIGHTING IS ALREADY HERE

Not long ago, saving electricity through lighting became all the rage through a new technology called compact fluorescent lighting (CFL). These spiral bulbs took over after a relatively short adoption period during which people often disliked the bluish hue that was given off by many of the models. These bulbs promised much higher lifetimes than incandescent bulbs averaging around 5000 hours and used one-fourth the power of an equivalent output incandescent light. Implementing these innovative bulbs has saved millions of tons of greenhouse gases from being generated by producing electricity for lighting. Other than the bulbs not living up to their projected lifetime, there is a downside to these bulbs. CFL bulbs contain mercury, which is toxic to humans and animals alike. Therefore, if you currently have these bulbs, please be sure to recycle them at your local hardware store when they burn out.

Further efficiencies in lighting are now being achieved using Light Emitting Diodes, or LED lights. LEDs have had a difficult time getting market acceptance due to their initial high price; however, the technology is quickly maturing, causing LED bulbs prices to drop significantly. Alternating current powered LEDs can still be expensive when compared to incandescent and CFL bulbs but they definitely have advantages. LED lighting uses approximately half of the power of the compact fluorescent or one-eighth the power of an equivalent output incandescent light. Even at the current price point, using *LED bulbs is a cost-effective way to improve your efficiency* and should be implemented prior to investing in photovoltaic panels if you are considering building to net zero, selling power to your local utility or living off of the grid.

These bulbs also have the distinct advantage that they last approximately 50,000 hours, or 10 times as long as the projected life of a CFL bulb. This 50,000 hour power rating is also based on the bulb maintaining 70 percent of its initial brightness; therefore, these bulbs will likely produce sufficient light for much longer than 50,000 hours. If you have difficulty believing that these bulbs will not last for the projected lifetime, then look at the time on your radio alarm clock, microwave, DVD player or stove; remember that those numbers are being displayed using LED lights, which have probably been on for several years.[81]

LEDs now come in many different colours and light output levels and are even customizable for ambience and entertainment purposes. LED bulbs are ideally suited for difficult-to-reach locations or where lights stay on for long periods. They can save considerable time, energy and maintenance expense as a result of their long life and reduced power consumption compared to CFLs or incandescent lights. LED bulbs have the further benefit that they don't produce heat, so if you live in a hot climate, implementing the bulbs will save you significant money on your cooling costs over time.

While retrofitting an existing building with LED lighting may be expensive in some applications, great opportunity exists in new construction for implementing LED lighting.

If the building is brand-new, LEDs have the benefit of potentially using direct current and hence smaller diameter wiring for implementing LED lighting solutions due to their low power consumption.

Since LEDs operate using DC current and the majority of the cost associated with LED bulbs is to transform standard AC voltage to DC voltage, the price of DC LED bulbs is generally lower. Additionally, the cost of installation should be lower, as a smaller gauge wire will be required for their installation. This saves money both on the device itself and on the expensive copper required to install the device. What's more, LED lighting is well-suited for homes or buildings that are powered using solar panels and batteries. The only real downside to this, however, is that currently electrical code in your jurisdiction may not approve of wiring using DC, and there may be a knowledge gap between the electricians and designers who would be installing or designing these systems. If wired for DC current using smaller gauge wiring, the installation of incandescent lighting is not possible as higher wattage lights would damage the wire and cause fires. For this reason, any lights that are wired with less than 14 gauge copper should be labeled as LED only. Caution: There are limits regarding the length of DC wiring which must be followed closely for any DC circuit. Consult your local electrical codes for details regarding these lengths and any other restrictions.

IF YOU ALREADY PAID FOR IT, REUSE IT

Remember when I was discussing HRVs and how they take the heat from exhaust air and transfer it to incoming cold air? The same type of heat recovery is possible using a relatively new technology called "drain water heat recovery." Since domestic hot water usage within a typical Canadian home accounts for approximately 30 percent of natural gas use within that household, why not recapture that heat and reuse it automatically? This is what the drain water heat recovery unit does.

The technology is a manufactured unit which consists of a standard size drain, with a coiled copper pipe that is wrapped around the drain. These devices are typically connected to the drain line from a shower or other grey water device (non-toilet) and to the cold water service line coming into the home. The function of the coil copper pipe is to run cold service water through it as the heated drain water goes through the drain section of the device. When someone is in the shower, the hot water running through the drain transfers its heat to the cold water service line, which is a coil that is surrounding the drain. This preheated service water is then plumbed directly to the cold faucet of the shower, which reduces the need for hot water provided from the hot water source. This preheating also has the benefit of stabilizing the water temperature in the shower and preventing the water temperature from creeping as the shower progresses.

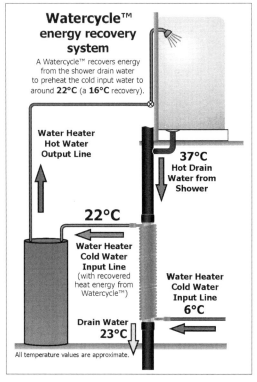

A diagram describing drain water heat recovery as depicted on the "watercycle" website.[82]

HERE COMES THE SUN... BE READY FOR IT

Solar panels, appropriately called PV panels, get a lot of press as being a sexy, green technology... and with good reason. Harnessing electricity from an endlessly renewable power supply is about as "green" as a device can get. The problem for most people is price... that is, for the time being.

As mentioned earlier, the price of photovoltaics has dropped significantly in the past years and is expected to continue to drop into the future. This means that in the near future, renewable energy via solar will be as cheap as existing electrical capacity as generated by coal and nuclear. By many accounts, this could happen as soon as 2020 for places that currently rely on cheap coal. In some locations photovoltaic electricity is already on par with the price of existing electrical utility power. In the book *Abundance*, Peter Diamandis and Steven Kotler discuss many energy scenarios that could revolutionize the future. One statistic that stands out in the book is that, the entire world could be 100 percent powered by solar by 2030 if driven strictly by economics alone. In other words, *if solar continues to grow on its own without government intervention, either for or against the industry, the whole world could be powered by 2030 using only the sun*.

Essentially, the missing key to wide spread implementation of solar is the upgrading of the current (and some would say rapidly decaying and outdated) power grid infrastructure to that of a Smart Grid. Without getting into the details of how a Smart Grid operates, consider that every building could now be its own power plant and networked together to all the rest of the buildings (power plants) constantly managing and distributing power as needed. When implemented correctly, a Smart Grid would be far more robust and efficient than the current electrical infrastructure because there would be far more power producers that are all interconnected together in a manner similar to how the Internet routes data. Upgrading to a Smart Grid and adding sufficient battery and distributed supplemental power generation would allow society to have cleaner power generated through several distributed sources, which would inherently improve efficiency. The alternative is to continue depending on a centralized power plant system which generally has significant losses due to transmission, high capital costs to construct and requires expensive fuel from an air quality and climate perspective.

With this in mind, being ready to become your own power plant and install photovoltaic panels should become a priority.

WHY NOT BE READY FOR WHEN YOU WANT TO INSTALL SOLAR?

In many jurisdictions such as in Vancouver, it is now code for new construction to have two conduits (1 ½ inch or 2 inch) or an empty electrical box ran to the underside of the roof to accommodate the electrical wiring necessary to install PV on the roof. Having conduits also allows for the future installation of solar thermal for use with domestic hot water or potentially for space heating. This simple consideration while the building is being constructed is cheap and extremely easy compared to drilling a hole through an existing insulated wall and then sealing and weather proofing that penetration. Since a builder or initial owner may not be able to or choose to install PV when the house is built, they might as well future proof the house for solar. Therefore, when owners choose to make the investment to free themselves from the power company (or become a power company themselves), the ability to do so is cheap, easy and relatively painless. Simply be sure to seal the penetrations from heat transfer and animal entry and label the conduits "solar ready" for future reference.

To make your home solar ready you should have a south-facing roof area that is preferably un-shaded and will remain that way for many years. If possible, choose to build your home in this way prior to design and before signing the building plans for your new home.

Recommendations

1. Super-insulate your house using one of the methods described to eliminate thermal bridging and reduce air leakage to the greatest extent possible. High-efficiency buildings should have at least R30 walls but shoot for R50 if it is within your means. The EQuillibrium homes target R24 under the floor by using 5 inches of extruded polystyrene, but a single R7 sheet of rigid on the exterior is better than nothing. R60 in the ceiling is recommended as a minimum and can be achieved with 24 inches of blown-in cellulose.

2. If you can purchase a lot that faces south, build with a passive solar design by orienting the long side of the building east to west, sizing windows properly and incorporating thermal mass into the structure. Be sure to not over-glaze by using too many windows or windows that are overused on the north, east and west sides of the building. This will prevent heat loss in the winter and heat gain in the summer. Opt for triple pane windows on all sides except south-facing, if money is an issue. Windows with a high solar heat gain coefficient (>.55) should be used in the south. These can be double-pane windows if necessary but should be triple-pane if budget allows.

3. Reduce the energy usage in your home by purchasing high-efficiency appliances and using LED lighting wherever possible.

4. Ensure that your building has adequate ventilation by having a properly sized and balanced heat recovery

ventilator or other means of ventilation installed. Having lots of house plants is another excellent option that can reduce the need for ventilation when there are few occupants.

5. Solar ready your home by taking the steps described in the solar section so that when the price of photovoltaic panels drops it will be easy for you to install them in your own home.

6. Reuse heat waste by installing drain water heat recovery systems.

7. If possible, use renewable energy such as ground source heat pumps, solar thermal, air-to-air heat pumps or wood heat to satisfy heating loads. These technologies will be discussed in later publications.

8. When burning wood, be sure to have sufficient combustion air to prevent backdrafts and smoke from entering the living space.

9. Incorporate natural ventilation via user-operated windows into the home design for use during summer months.

10. Prior to moving in, commission the building envelope using a certified thermographer to check for cold spots and problems with the insulation. Have a comprehensive inspection completed to ensure that components and systems were installed and are operating correctly.

11. If you live in the prairies, install a sump pump in your basement. The water table is rising and if you can't get rid of that water, you will have a major financial problem and potential health risk on your hands.

12. Shade the area around your home and put up wind breaks on the north, east and west to reduce the heat loss in the winter time via wind loading.

13. Avoid using carpets within the home, as they trap dust and dirt and often release volatile organic compounds (VOCs).

14. Avoid using paints, sealants and building materials that release VOCs.

15. Install water efficient appliances such as dual flush toilets and water aeration devices in faucets to reduce water usage.

16. Capture rain water in rain barrels or direct it away from the foundation of your home and of your neighbour's home to prevent the potential for basement flooding.

17. Direct people to www.futureproofmybuilding.com so that they can learn this information and benefit from it as well.

18. Stay tuned to www.futureproofmybuilding.com to learn more as I am able to add to this information in future blog posts, videos and newsletters.

THE LIST GOES ON

This book touches on the most important aspects of building green and reducing your energy dependence in a cold climate. There are so many more technologies, strategies and aspects that are involved in being truly sustainable, green, environmental or future proof. I will be blogging about these issues, discussing other technologies and identifying opportunities for job creation, sustainability and creating security within our society in the coming months.

I value your feedback, so if you have an opinion about this content or you would like to learn more, please send me an email at info@futureproofmybuilding.com.

Please watch for my newsletter, stay tuned to my blog and share this book and my content with your family, friends, colleagues and anyone who is building a house or is involved in construction by sending them to www.futureproofmybuilding.com. Change occurs when people understand that there is a better way to do things and we all work in that direction.

Additionally, I recognize that many readers may have already been familiar with the concepts within this publication. If not, then great! I sincerely hope that my effort was of great value and benefit to you and that you use this information to reduce your energy dependence by seeking out those individuals who are already implementing the techniques and strategies discussed herein.

If you are a designer, contractor, builder or distributor of the goods and services discussed in this publication: I want to help you reach your customers! That is why I have gone to great effort and expense to write this book and to have a website and database created to connect customers to the people and products that can truly make a positive environmental impact. You can register at: www.futureproofmybuilding.com/register

Acknowledgements

Special thanks go to Dr. Rob Dumont for sharing the knowledge and insight he has amassed from studying this topic over the last 40 years. Without his help and guidance, this work would not be possible.

Thanks to my lovely lady Deb, for her hard work, love, support and patience while starting this business and while putting in the groundwork for creating the future proof community. Thanks go out to my parents Wayne and Lillian for their love and support. Şerefe (cheers) to my awesome roommate Bahir Sokmenoglu for not getting upset that I work at the kitchen table from time to time.

Thanks to Daeren Gall for starting a conversation with me at River Landing on a sunny day in May and showing me that complete strangers can begin to collaborate based on good faith and a hunch that we can make the world a better place. Thanks to Michael Leydon of Springboard West, who has been of great help to me both in providing feedback for this book and in helping me to start the web service that will bring all of the concepts within this book together.

Thanks to Kari Calder for her insights into the housing market in Saskatoon. Also big thanks to Rodney Carter for his insights into the quickly evolving field of LED lighting.

Thanks to my friends Vince Anderson, Graham Dickson and Mike Nemeth for their time spent reviewing this work. Your feedback has been most helpful.

Thanks to my colleagues at Integrated Designs for their insight and shared enthusiasm for building green.

And thank you from me and from future generations for sharing this message and for implementing the principles, techniques and technologies discussed within this book.

Resources

Canadian Home Builders' Association Builders' Manual. Ottawa: Canadian Home Builders' Association, 2008. Print.

Diamandis, Peter H., and Steven Kotler. Abundance: The Future Is Better than You Think. New York: Free, 2012. Print.

Lovins, Amory B. Reinventing Fire: Bold Business Solutions for the New Energy Era. White River Junction, VT: Chelsea Green Pub., 2011. Print.

Solplan Review – The independent journal of energy conservation, building science and construction practice. For information or subscription contact solplan@shaw.ca

Solplan Review 146 (May 2009): n. pag. Print.

Solplan Review 153 (August 2010): n. pag. Print.

Solplan Review 162 (January 2012): n. pag. Print.

Solplan Review 163 (March 2012): n. pag. Print.

Concrete CO2 Fact Sheet Feb 2012. N.p., Feb. 2012. Web. 10 Sept. 2012. <http://www.nrmca.org/sustainability/CONCRETE%20 CO2%20FACT%20SHEET%20FEB%202012.pdf>.

"EQuilibrium ™ Sustainable Housing Demonstration Initiative." EQuilibrium ™ Housing. N.p., n.d. Web. 27 Oct. 2012. <http://www. cmhc-schl.gc.ca/en/co/maho/yohoyohe/heho/eqho/index.cfm>.

"Insulating Your House." Canada Mortgage and Housing. N.p., n.d. Web. 27 Nov. 2012. <http://www.cmhc.ca/en/co/maho/enefcosa/ enefcosa_002.cfm>.

Ortlepp, Angelika. "Top Ten Secrets of a Successful Home Design." N.p., n.d. Web.

"R Value Chart." R-Value Table. N.p., n.d. Web. 20 Sept. 2012. <http:// www.allwallsystem.com/design/RValueTable.html>.

Average Temperature Calculations were made using: http://saskatoon. weatherstats.ca/metrics/hdd.html

"Passive Solar Building Design." Wikipedia. Wikimedia Foundation, 27 Nov. 2012. Web. 27 Nov. 2012. <http://en.wikipedia.org/wiki/ Passive_solar_building_design>.

"North America Residential Building Code Resource Center."
Residential Building Code Resource Center. N.p., n.d. Web. 5 Sept.
2012. <http://building.dow.com/na/en/tools/codes.htm>.

NOTES

1   As determined by British efficiency research David Olivier. Discussed in Home Energy (magazine), May/June 2000.

2   R-value is the imperial measure of thermal resistance, which North Americans tend to be more familiar with. The metric and thus worldwide version of R-value is RSI, which will not be used as reference in this publication.

3   If you look back at older homes, you can see this evolution over time, which basically correlates to the price of energy. Prior to the 1970s, a 2x4 wall insulated to R14 was considered sufficient in Canada. During the energy crisis of the 1970s many people began to implement a much higher standard with the advent of double wall construction. But since energy prices dropped in the 1980s, a lesser standard has been adopted. Hence, we see that a 2x6 wall is considered sufficient by most at the present time.

4   The proposed changes are approximately on par with the R2000 standard or will meet Energuide 80. This situation is complicated because Energuide now has a new format.

5   Currently you can build a minimally insulated glass fortress in even the coldest of climates. As long as you can size the mechanical equipment sufficiently to heat and cool the building during the expected high and low temperature within that region, then you are allowed to build it with the existing legislation. This current lack of regulation takes no account into consideration that this structure will use energy throughout its lifetime. When one drives through any city in Canada and sees the minimally insulated/glass facade high rises, chain stores and box stores that are designed and constructed simply for purposes of brand identity, it is this lack of regulation that allows this. Keep in mind that these stores are often architecturally designed for climates such as California, which are much less harsh than those of the Canadian prairies. Thankfully there are many professionals like myself who would like to see this circumstance changed.

6   I suspect Canada would rank even lower if compared to several of the Nordic countries. "Canada Ranks 2nd-last in Energy Efficiency Study." CBC News. 16 July 2012. Web. http://www.cbc.ca/news/technology/story/2012/07/16/energy-scorecard.html

7   One percent of 7,000,000,000 people in the world is 70,000,000.
     Though there are many people in Russia, Greenland, Iceland,
     Norway, Sweden, the northern United States and a few other Nordic
     countries who would experience a similar climate, it is a safe bet that
     we deal with much colder conditions.

8   Source: "IEA World Energy Outlook 2012: U.S. To Be
     Energy Independent; Subsidies To Fossil Fuels Worth $523
     Billion." The Full. N.p., n.d. Web. 20 Nov. 2012. <http://www.
     huffingtonpost.ca/2012/11/12/iea-us-top-oil-producer-fossil-fuel-
     subsidies_n_2117727.html?utm_hp_ref=canada-business>.

9   Yearly average temperatures were calculated by using the
     average of each month and dividing by 12. Source http://www.
     theweathernetwork.com/statistics/cl4057180

10   Overheating in the summer is also readily caused by un-shaded
     windows. According to Rob Dumont, on a sunny day, an un-shaded
     window can take in 200btu per hour per square foot. By comparison
     an R50 wall has a very low heat transfer through it.

11   This is an aside that I added on September 12, when it was 5°C and
     the furnace came on several times in my fiancés house. This is a new
     house that was built in 2007. Rob Dumont's house, by comparison,
     doesn't usually require an external source of heating until late
     October, when daytime temperatures are usually much lower and
     overnight temperatures have been dipping much colder for much
     longer.

12   According to a press release from the Saskatchewan Party dated June
     2012, 23,632 housing starts occurred in Saskatchewan since 2007.

13   Many scientists all over the world have been talking about this for
     decades and I'm not going to cite anyone in particular. If you have
     doubt regarding the legitimacy of climate change then please watch
     this video: http://www.ted.com/talks/james_hansen_why_i_must_
     speak_out_about_climate_change.html

14   If you don't believe me, you probably haven't experienced smog,
     sat in traffic for long enough or been disappointed that you can no
     longer eat the fish in your favourite lake. Or perhaps you just have
     not been paying attention.

15   According to an ASHRAE presentation I attended in October
     of 2012, every dollar spent on energy efficiency is the equivalent
     of six dollars spent on renewable energy sources with regards to
     moving towards net zero building. This should be the goal of all new
     construction.

16 By this I am referring to the propaganda that we are fed concerning the rate at which fossil fuel resources should be exploited rather than focusing on what we can do to reduce our dependence on these limited and polluting commodities.

17 See Rob Dumont's biography at the beginning of this book. He was able to do this in 1992 before the solar thermal industry created the technology that he uses to offset his heating requirements.

18 Source: http://www.greenbuildingadvisor.com/blogs/dept/green-architects-lounge/photovoltaics-part-2-enter-dollar?utm_source=email&utm_medium=eletter&utm_content=20120921-new-business&utm_campaign=fine-homebuilding-building-business

19 A great blog article that explains this phenomenon accompanies the chart. Chart used with permission from: http://rameznaam.com/2011/03/17/the-exponential-gains-in-solar-power-per-dollar/

20 Source: http://unbridledspeculation.com/2011/03/17/the-exponential-gains-in-solar-power-per-dollar

21 "Reinventing Fire" by Amory B Lovins provides a roadmap of how society can be free of Fossil Fuels and Nuclear energy by 2050 while growing the economy by 158 percent. A great TED talk about the subject is located here: http://www.ted.com/talks/amory_lovins_a_50_year_plan_for_energy.html

22 A great blog article that explains this phenomenon accompanies the chart. Chart used with permission from: http://rameznaam.com/2011/03/17/the-exponential-gains-in-solar-power-per-dollar/

23 I wrote an article concerning how we should be thinking long-term with our power sources. It was published here: http://www.thestarphoenix.com/Think+long+term+power+source/6920899/story.html

24 Facts about the ice storm summarized from: http://canadaonline.about.com/cs/weather/p/icestorm.htm

25 Source: http://www.pikeresearch.com/research/natural-gas-trucks-and-buses

26 There are many articles on this, but consider: http://asiancorrespondent.com/76124/japans-natural-gas-boom-and-what-it-means-to-you/

27 Watch the trailer for Gasland here: http://www.youtube.com/
watch?v=z0fAsFQsFAs. Also read about how these wells are
not putting out the expected gas returns here: http://www.
huffingtonpost.com/brendan-demelle/fracking-output_b_1900810.
html

28 The major component of natural gas is methane, which has 20 times
the global warming potential of CO_2.

29 This link is to a study conducted by the Canadian Mortgage and
Housing Corporation (CMHC) discussing how to retrofit existing
buildings to be energy efficient. The paper also discusses paybacks,
which are far less favourable then doing it right from the start. http://
www.cmhc-schl.gc.ca/odpub/pdf/67629.pdf?fr=1346874396828

30 MMBTU is the abbreviation for 1,000,000 Btu or British Thermal
Units. A Btu is approximately the amount of energy needed to heat 1
pound (0.454 kg) of water, which is exactly one tenth of a UK gallon
or about 0.1198 US gallons, from 39 °F to 40 °F (3.8 °C to 4.4 °C).

31 There are many places to find this data. An image on the web that
shows prices in cents per cubic meter which is typical of many
energy bills is here: http://myrateenergy.ca/images/graph-gas.jpg.
I have revamped an image created from the data on the following
website to demonstrate Per MMBTU from: http://www.gasalberta.
com/pricing-market.htm. A conversion chart can be rendered using
data from here: http://www.infomine.com/investment/metal-prices/
natural-gas/1-year/

32 If this is a suburban expansion or new neighbourhood, then it also
requires new roads, new water delivery, new sewage infrastructure,
earth work for drainage etc. This continual expansion is encroaching
on nature and separates us further apart, which costs us even more
energy as we can travel to amenities we need and to our places of
work while also reducing the amount of free time we have due to
the time involved in commuting. This is why I discuss later that we
should be building upward to encourage better urban environments,
which are much more manageable and healthier for society.

33 I have chosen 100 units as an easy reference point for the sake of
easy illustration. Of course, every building uses a different amount
of energy based on its size, orientation, where it is built, its insulation
level, its occupant habits etc. The point is to illustrate that as our
economy grows, if we don't reduce our energy usage for everything
that is built new, then our dependence as a society increases.

34 Truth be told, this is already happening in the form of incentive programs to reduce the energy usage of existing buildings through programs like lighting retrofits and the EcoEnergy retrofit program. The economics behind these programs are due to the simple fact that it is cheaper, easier and healthier for the economy to reduce the existing demand than it is to create new supply.

35 At the time that Rob built his house, he created a solar thermal system using available materials for the collector and built a 1400L heat storage tank in his basement. His forced air system circulates solar heated water through a coil in the forced air system to temper incoming outdoor air. Since then, engineered solar thermal collectors are available on the market that could be used to create a more reliable and higher efficiency solar thermal system.

36 To read about Rob's home and see a breakdown of the incremental costs of the project, you can view the pdf describing his home here: http://www.futureproofmybuilding.com/rob-dumont-housenotes/

37 Photo from Fotolia

38 Such questions lead to other questions like: "What is missing in my life that I feel the need to collect stuff?", "Do I really pay attention to the marketing on TV?"

39 -10°C is a warm morning in March in Saskatchewan. The rate of heat transfer through an object increases as the difference in temperature between the two environments increases.

40 Heat flow is a very complicated process that occurs through conduction, convection and radiation. Heat loss through a wall is mostly through conduction and thus R-value plays the largest role next to air leakage.

41 This is true unless there is significant air leakage or thermal bridging that increases the heat loss in the winter. Heat gain in the summer would be mainly through un-shaded windows and heat radiated or conducted from the roof. Heat gain at any time of the year that is not through mechanical equipment is generally through un-shaded windows, electronics and people.

42 The R-value of a wall will depend on many factors including building size and cost. Typically a lower R-value is acceptable as the building size and number of occupants increase. People produce heat and hence this must be accounted for in larger buildings. A house has very few people to heat it per unit area compared to an office building, stadium or hospital, for example.

43 If you already own a home, grants and programs are likely available in your area to make improvements to your home accessible and cost–effective in the short to medium term. Over the long term, this is a great investment that reduces your expenses and adds value to your existing asset while also contributing to the local economy.

44 This is a generalised statement that applies to the greatest extent as the climate of the location gets colder. These technologies are great and are part of the solution, but they have been shown to be less cost–effective than superinsulation.

45 Source Solplan Review, May 2009. R-values vary by product. A more complete list is can be found later in this e-book or at: http://www.cmhc-schl.gc.ca/en/co/maho/enefcosa/enefcosa_002.cfm

46 Statistic taken from: http://www.sips.org/technical-information-2/thermal-performance/r-values/

47 These factors are dependent on the sizes of equipment available as well as on the energy requirements of your home.

48 Using electric heat is currently far more expensive than heating with natural gas in many areas that don't have access to cheap hydro-electricity. If photovoltaic panels are introduced to the project, then this cost can potentially be offset during the summer months.

49 If you are such a professional, please register with my service to connect with efficiency-minded customers at http://www.futureproofmybuilding.com/register.

50 A colleague in Saskatoon told me that this was done at her house. Check with your local building codes to see if this is applicable in your area. Ensure that the person who does the installation is certified if you choose to do this instead of using a poly vapour barrier.

51 Photo credit Gordon Howel: www.hme.ca. Some information from: http://www.vereco.ca/green_project_details.html?gid=12&gcat_id=6

52 Source: http://en.wikipedia.org/wiki/Insulating_concrete_form

53 Check your local codes regarding vapour barrier requirements.

54 Images used with permission from: http://nudura.com/en/divisions/contractors_builders/icf-prooducts.aspx

55 See Solplan Review, August 2010, p. 10, for a discussion of foam thickness issues.

56 Source: http://www.innovateus.net/innopedia/why-spray-foam-insulation-used

57   http://www.greenbuildingadvisor.com/green-basics/spray-foam-insulation-open-and-closed-cell

58   See Solplan Review, August 2010, p. 10, for a discussion on foam thickness issues.

59   Image Source: http://www.flickr.com/photos/30585638@N07/6804316372/

60   Image Source: http://www.flickr.com/photos/blizzardfx/2965038427/sizes/l/in/photostream/

61   Source: http://www.ecotecinsulation.com/spray_foam_insulation_benefits.html

62   Source: http://www.sprayfoam.com/spps/ahpg.cfm?spgid=1

63   Multiple sources, such as http://www.innovateus.net/innopedia/why-spray-foam-insulation-used and http://www.greenbuildingadvisor.com/green-basics/spray-foam-insulation-open-and-closed-cell

64   A comment noted from discussions with a spray foam professional with Poly Plus Insulators Inc.

65   Source: http://msdssearch.dow.com/PublishedLiteratureDOWCOM/dh_041f/0901b8038041f94a.pdf?filepath=styrofoam/pdfs/noreg/179-07577.pdf&fromPage=GetDoc

66   Alternatively mineral wool can be used around the basement foundation. Source: http://www.cmhc.ca/en/co/maho/enefcosa/enefcosa_002.cfm

67   Check with local codes and installation practises to ensure that this is permitted where you live.

68   This is discussed in thermography literature and is very evident when taking thermal graphic images. The problem is that the heat must be reflected back into the space but is going to be blocked by the drywall or wall barrier. Reflectivity values taken from http://www.measurement.sk/2004/S3/Bartl.pdf

69   Description is summarize from http://en.wikipedia.org/wiki/Structural_insulated_panel

70   Image used with permission. Photo credit Nick Eastman: http://www.eastmanhomes.com/index.php?option=com_content&view=article&id=48&Itemid=113

71   Outperform 2x4 http://www.sips.org/technical-information-2/thermal-performance/r-values/

72 SIPS chart data taken from: http://www.fischersips.com/about/r-value. I question these values as performing in the real world vs. in a lab setting, but provide them as reference.

73 Windows are typically thermally rated using U values where U is the symbol for heat flow. To calculate the R-value of windows you are selecting, simply take the inverse of the U value. R =1/U or U = 1/R. High-efficiency window information from: http://www.efficientwindows.org/ufactor.cfm

74 In a super-insulated house with good solar access and high thermal mass, this number is likely to be much higher, though the heat load is dependent on the outdoor air temperature, location and time of year.

75 For a free guide to understanding Passive Solar Design for window sizing and to potentially hire Saskatchewan based experts in Passive Solar Design, visit www.howtousesolar.com

76 Image credit: http://greenpassivesolar.com/passive-solar/scientific-principles/movement-of-the-sun/

77 Source: http://www.eere.energy.gov/de/passive_solar_design.html

78 Information taken from Solplan Review, August 2010.

79 Most HRV models do not allow for connection to exhaust range hoods.

80 This is one of the reasons that photovoltaic energy is great. It is available when the highest electrical load is present.

81 Note that these LEDs use less power and therefore may have a different lifespan as a result.

82 Image used with permission from: http://www.watercycles.ca/

83 One could argue that this is already the case in Alberta. Prices for electrical production are posted here: http://ets.aeso.ca/ The argument is based on a discussion in the article: http://www.greenbuildingadvisor.com/blogs/dept/green-architects-lounge/photovoltaics-part-2-enter-dollar?utm_source=email&utm_medium=eletter&utm_content=20120921-new-business&utm_campaign=fine-homebuilding according t according to zo-building-business

7402321R00073

Made in the USA
San Bernardino, CA
04 January 2014